A SEEKER'S GUIDE TO A
LIFE WORTH LIVING

In her new book Jili Hamilton makes it clear she is a master teacher. The depth of the well from which she draws her wisdom is unfathomable because she is so deeply rooted in Infinite Presence. There seems to be no area of one's life in which she is not able to offer insights, inspiration and motivation. I love this book because the writings are, each unto their own, tasty, profound and easy-to-assimilate tidbits of truth. If you are serious in your intent to create a life truly worth living, this is a book you will want to read, perhaps more than once.
Dennis Merritt Jones, author of *The Art of Uncertainty: How to Live in the Mystery of Life and Love*

Jili Hamilton has done her homework—and more! *A Seeker's Guide* is a wonderful and wise companion on our own journey. It's packed with powerful spiritual principles, sparkling insights and—best of all—illustrative stories we can all relate to. Hamilton goes the extra mile to show just how unpredictable and worthwhile each day can be if we stay awake.
Carol Adrienne PhD, author of *The Purpose of Your Life*

In this book Jili expresses in one sentence that which we all should take note of: 'We are capable of far more than we imagine.' This is a work of considerable depth and under-standing. It suggests that it is the striving for power and money with no thought for others that creates a flaw through and by which we are constantly defeated. It teaches us to discover peace, knowledge and sharing which will bring harmony; and ultimately, through this, we will find success. In Jili's words: 'When we work to light the path for others, we light our own path.'

George Alexanda, author of *Birch: The Beginning*

I have known Jili for many years, during which time she has been an inspiration to many people. She is a very spiritual person and has spread many gems of wisdom during the years. Long may she continue to do so.

Kate Lawrence, Holistic Healers Association

A Seeker's Guide
to a Life
worth Living

A Seeker's Guide to a Life worth Living

Jili Hamilton

BOOKS

Winchester, UK
Washington, USA

First published by O-Books, 2013
O-Books is an imprint of John Hunt Publishing Ltd., Laurel House, Station Approach,
Alresford, Hants, SO24 9JH, UK
office1@jhpbooks.net
www.johnhuntpublishing.com

For distributor details and how to order please visit the 'Ordering' section on our website.

Text copyright: Jili Hamilton 2013

ISBN: 978 1 78279 118 8

A CIP catalogue record for this book is available from the British Library.

Design: Stuart Davies

Printed in the USA by Edwards Brothers Malloy

We operate a distinctive and ethical publishing philosophy in all
areas of our business, from our global network of authors to
production and worldwide distribution.

CONTENTS

Introduction

It was in the spring of 2011 that I was told I was going to write a book.

'I've already written one,' I replied.

'Well, you're going to write another one; in fact you're going to write three more and you'll know when you've finished,' countered the other person. 'You're going to start the next one very soon.'

'But I don't know what to write about,' I protested.

'You will,' he assured me, 'you will.'

All through that summer I was very busy with other jobs and although the notion of a book floated around now and then, I still had no idea about how to start or what to write.

I finished all my work contracts in November 2011 and then flew to London to visit the Festival for Mind, Body, Spirit. On walking in the door, the first stand I encountered was that of a small online weekly magazine, and, ever anxious to promote what I do as a complementary therapist working with ear treatment candles, I asked if they would publish an article I had written about them.

'With pleasure,' the guy on the stand told me.

Monday morning, back home, I submitted my text. The editor must have liked the style or something about it and I was invited to write a regular column for the magazine. I accepted gladly and the ideas came pouring out. Any distraction that took me away from writing was unwelcome and within two or three months, anecdotes of all sorts had come flooding back to me, examples on which I could base a whole series of little stories. I wanted to offer something that anyone could relate to—perhaps even those who had never given a thought as to how they could change their lives—and I'm not saying that this book provides the answer to all their questions. My mission is to set out ideas, *possibilities*, based on my own experience of how things changed in my own life; how they changed for other people I knew; and through the examples and the simple suggestions I make, how they can work for you, the reader.

This, therefore, is one of the books I was told I would write. The subjects are many and varied and I have changed the names of the people whom I've known or know personally and whose stories I have used. The idea is for you to dip in and choose one that appeals to you, or to read through the book systematically. The chapters are all relatively short so you can pick it up when you've only a few minutes to spare; you can turn to a story that has a particular message at a given moment. The texts can also be used as a basis for discussion groups. I'm sure you will find the method that best suits you.

Whichever way you choose, if you have half the pleasure using the book that I had writing it, then my goal has certainly been met.

Jili

Author of:
Messages from beyond the Veil
Ear Treatment Candles (an updated version of *Hopi Candles*)

Acknowledgments

I owe a great debt to my teachers who over the years have shown me a different way of looking at the world. I thank every one of them, especially those who gave me a hard time.

I am grateful for the teachings of the New Thought movement and for those who have been involved for many years in passing on its precepts in the form of books, workshops, conferences, etc.

My gratitude goes, too, to all those people who have crossed my path, either fleetingly or who have spent more time with me and who figure in the book. They have also been powerful teachers and although their names have been changed, I'll never forget the lessons they brought.

Thanks also go to PaTrisha-Anne Todd who has pointed out places where ideas needed to be clearer, helped me to keep my opinions out of the text and added the benefit of her experience to give a better, sharper focus to the contents.

SECTION 1: Abundance

Abundance

So much has already been written and said about abundance and how to achieve it. There have been workshops and books galore on the subject, because in our material world we are told that having more money (and that's what abundance means to many of us) is the only way to enjoy a fun-filled and successful life.

It can of course mean having more money, but that's not all there is to it. A good few years ago I came across this word and it gave me ideas of being wealthier, too. Time went by. I evolved and my ideas changed, causing me to have a radical rethink about my concept of abundance. Now I can see that it's truly a remarkable state of being.

For some it might not mean more money—it could mean having less—but that's not what it's about at all. Many of us have grown up being told that money doesn't grow on trees, although I often think that as banknotes are paper, made from trees, perhaps money does!

And what about us?

Let's take a look at what's going on in our lives.

Health: abundance could mean sparkling health, and once we possess this priceless commodity, we can savor an abundance of joy in all we do and in every other aspect of the life we lead.

For those of us who are self-employed, abundance can mean plenty of work; for those of us who are rushed off our feet it can mean more time to chill out and smell the roses. For those of us who are in financial straits, it could indeed lead to getting out of debt and raising our earning power.

Taking into consideration other angles of our life, it could mean more invitations out for a meal with friends, family, colleagues; perhaps someone sharing the produce of their garden; being offered free tickets to a concert; someone giving us a book. Abundance has so many ways in which to express itself.

How can we make it work?

Now that we know what abundance can mean, how do we lock into it?

Well, for me it started about 20 years ago. I had always been terrified of spending money, of not having enough, so abundance workshops seemed to be the answer to my worries. For quite a while I still thought of abundance as having more money, not necessarily to spend—let's not be rash—but more to put in the bank where it could pile up in peace. I hadn't understood that the first Principle of Abundance is not receiving more and more, but *giving* more and more, and that when we give we are sending out a message that we still have plenty where that came from.

Giving takes many forms. This could be money, time, help, a little treat to cheer a friend going through a tough time, just something to say: 'I'm thinking of you'; it certainly doesn't have to be a lot and, well, I'm sure some of you could add ideas of your own to the list. Once I had understood that what you give out comes back, I started to get the hang of this Universal Law.

In spite of this, I still wasn't quite there. I finally worked out that abundance is when you give *without thinking* of what, if anything, you'll receive back; that's when you start to get the message. I often find that if I do something for someone, I receive something good from someone completely different. Here's a tip I learnt at a workshop and which I find useful: on the back of every check I write the phrase *Money circulates freely in my life*. It flows in and it flows out; that's what money is meant to do.

There's a saying that someone once shared with me about how money is like manure: keep it in a big pile and it smells, but spread it around and it makes the flowers grow.

It isn't giving and receiving that matters as much as putting a message out into the ethers that we have plenty to spare and to share, and when something *does* come back to us, whatever it may be and from whatever source, let's not forget to say 'thank you', not only to the person doing the giving but to the universal energy through which we are all connected.

As Others See Us

Towards the end of a weekend workshop in which I participated, we all had to pair up and write a list of adjectives which we felt described our partner. We were then to share with each other what we'd written.

I remember little of what I said about my partner but she had written all kinds of adjectives about me that I didn't relate to at all. They were along the lines of 'earth mother' and that is about as far as you can get from the image I (or anyone else for that matter) had of me.

The mirror effect

Once we'd finished sharing, the facilitator told us to exchange our lists because we had really been talking about ourselves. He explained that what we see and feel in others, or what we think we see and feel, is something that resonates with a quality or fault we have. All the adjectives my partner had applied to me described her very well. And vice versa.

It's true that some people press our buttons every time we clap eyes on them.

If we keep coming across people who seem to us to have the same irritating habit, then it pays dividends to look more closely at our own reactions to things. It can be very painful because we're convinced we're not like that. Until we can see that *is* the way we function, we are unlikely to make any change.

What does this tell us about ourselves?

Sometimes we can see another person's foibles so clearly and we smile as we realize that could have been a good description of the way we were at one time, but we understand that we don't react like that anymore so we have probably dealt with it. We can meet people in social situations and find nothing in common at all with their views and values, which leave us completely indifferent. Understanding that it works both ways, we don't seek out each other's company.

We can also look around at the people we do like and who seem to like to be around us. That works because we've probably got common interests, or a compatible sense of humor, and, sometimes when we're very much on the same wavelength, we have the same thoughts at the same time.

While running stands at exhibitions in London I loved working with a particular friend, John. We could often anticipate what the other was going to say and we shared the same philosophy on working together. He could also be quite blunt with me whenever stress got the upper hand. We didn't have very much else in common but workwise we were completely compatible.

Building our self-esteem

A work colleague and I once had a conversation about how some of our co-workers ended up over and over again with bullying bosses who gave them a hard time. We had a mutual friend who always seemed to have to stay late for no good reason and much of her working day was spent doing personal work for her boss. We talked about violence in a partnership, too, and we both agreed that, although we had never experienced it ourselves, some women seemed to attract only violent or uncaring boyfriends. Now whether it's a bad boss or a violent partner, many people have come to understand that one person is holding a mirror up to the other and it's all about self-esteem or the lack of it: if we have little or no self-esteem, we may very well consider that someone who doesn't respect us by treating us with proper consideration is acceptable.

How others help us

By ourselves, we can rarely see the need to improve some aspects of our personality, but when someone we like and trust is able to point it out to us and we are able to accept their criticism, it's a great gift and can help us to move on.

Scotland's national poet Robert Burns had a very romantic way of putting it and I can never read his poem 'To a Louse' without being totally in agreement when he, too, expresses the thought that, if we were given the power to see ourselves as others see us, it would certainly free us from many blunders and foolish notions.

Attachment and Detachment

Several years ago while living in London I took a course entitled You Can Heal Your Life, given by two people who had studied with Louise Hay, its originator, in the USA.

We met every week for a couple of months and I remember little about it except for a particular incident. One week a participant arrived and burst into tears saying that her boyfriend had dumped her and she was devastated. The advice she was given was to try and let him go. Very difficult to do, but to try and let him go with love and in that way cut the tie. The following week she came back saying that she'd tried that and he had called, told her he had made a mistake and asked her to give him another chance.

We are told that if we love something we should let it go free and if it does 'belong' to us it will come back. If it doesn't, then it belongs somewhere else: a timely reminder that neediness in a relationship will likely attract an undesirable outcome.

Easing the pain

How hard it is to let go when we badly want something that doesn't want us. If we can manage to do it we save ourselves untold pain in two ways. The first is that, well, it could come back to us once we put out the message that it's OK to let go, and the second is that we certainly save tears, months, years, and driving all our friends crazy if it isn't going to return and we can manage to relax our grip.

I don't mean that if we can't be with the person we want to be with we immediately look around for someone else, because every type of loss needs a period of grieving and healing, whether it's the physical death of a near-and-dear or the end of a relationship or friendship. We need to be able to reach a certain closure and, looking at it from a logical point of view, it's a waste of time trying to hang on because, if it is the end, then we must acknowledge that change is a fact of life and however painful and however much we don't want to, we must move on to something else.

I once worked with Christiane, a mother of two little girls, and she, too, was devastated when her husband decided that the responsibility of a family was something he didn't feel capable of continuing. He took a tiny apartment in the same small town and their children saw him very frequently. Little by little, my colleague got over her initial pain, detached herself from her husband and found certain advantages in being on her own. Her immediate work colleagues were a sociable lot and she had plenty of opportunities to get out and about. I didn't see her to speak too much for quite a while as we worked in different buildings, but, at a party I gave on leaving the company, she told me that her husband had wanted them to get back together as a family but she felt it was too late. She and her daughters were returning to her home city several hundred miles away to start a new life.

Picking up the pieces

When things have worked out, people have sometimes got back together, even remarried—perhaps older and wiser and feeling much stronger thanks to what went before—but we have to accept the fact that detaching and freeing the other with love is the best thing to do as a start and, if we are meant to be with a particular person, we then go back on our own terms.

It's a bit like breaking a leg. At first there is the agony of the break, then the hobbling around with crutches and a plaster for several weeks. There's nothing we can do to speed things up so we have to make the best of it. And then, once the healing is complete, we wake up one day and realize that we can go dancing again.

Counting Our Blessings

It's so easy to get into the widespread doom and gloom that people seem really to enjoy sharing with us. If we read the mainstream press and watch television, there is very little good news, news that makes us feel lucky to be alive. It is said that bad news makes for higher sales, and the publication *Positive News*, which only prints positive articles and has stayed a marginal newspaper rather than a best-seller, tends to bear this out.

What is it about us that makes us want to lock into the negative side of life? Is it because we enjoy thinking that we're at least better off than the cases reported in the media? Does this make us feel superior in some way? I find it pulls me down so I've put a stop to reading newspapers or listening to the news.

We so often forget to count our many, many blessings and thinking things are going from bad to worse is a very uncomfortable way to live.

Another factor is that a belief that bad things are more likely to happen to us than good invariably draws them into our orbit and I remember being told that the incidence of lung cancer had increased when the warning started to appear on packets of cigarettes. People who hadn't realized that smoking was bad for their health were suddenly confronted with their worst fears.

When you're given lemons

It's interesting how people who seem to be in really difficult situations are the ones most likely to have a positive turn of mind and who tend to talk about the things for which they are grateful rather than expressing their woes. I have heard one or two stories of terminally ill patients in hospital, knowing that they haven't had long to live, who have been the ones to cheer up their friends and relatives. Hospices invariably have a very uplifting atmosphere and I'm sure so much of that comes from the letting go by the patients and the love and caring which pervades the whole place. When you know that your days are counted, you can truly be yourself and perhaps find the courage to tell people how much you have always loved them and what they've meant to you.

I once had an elderly neighbor in London whose Jewish parents had fled Germany in the 1930s when she was still a child. As a teenager she had had an accident in a swimming pool and as a result had great difficulty walking, even with two crutches. One day I mentioned that I had never heard her complain about the difficulties she had in doing so much that we take for granted. She explained that she was eternally grateful that she and her family had found a safe place to live and anything else that happened to her was just an inconvenience. She was happy to look after the spare door keys for many of the more forgetful residents, and I enjoyed spending time with her chatting about life in general.

On her mother's suggestion, she had taken up painting in her youth and had painted (and potted) until almost the end of her life. Several times we visited exhibitions together in the big London galleries and I learnt so much from her trained eye. There is a print of one of her paintings on the wall at home so I think about her often. She was someone who regularly counted her blessings; life had given her lemons and she made lemonade. And very good it was, too.

Events That Change Our Lives

If we look back I imagine we can all find plenty of life-changing events which have had a huge impact on our lives, although at the time they might have seemed totally insignificant and quickly forgotten. Visiting a new place, being hit by a tragedy or a sudden joyful occasion, even a comment from someone that has sent us chasing up a new path has perhaps changed our lives forever.

For me there have been so many but one I remember very clearly was when I was working in Glasgow and wanted to spend the summer working as a temporary secretary in London. I found somewhere to live and an agency found me jobs. With one of my first placements I ended up in a major advertising agency which handled the account of an important watchmaker based in Geneva. Never having been abroad much and not having had the courage to join friends who'd taken off for spells in Canada and Australia, when I was offered a job in Switzerland it seemed like a last chance. Suffice to say that even though I've lived on and off in other places in the interim, Switzerland has been my home for nearly half my life.

Turning points

One of the first people I got to know when I started work in Geneva was an Irish girl who went dancing with her friends every Saturday night. The guy who became her husband had gone to the same nightclub only once in his life and there they had met. Another girl I knew met her husband when he went to help her as she was struggling to get a bar of chocolate out of a machine at a railway station.

Yet another colleague, a Jewish girl, who worked with me for a short time, had been going out with a Catholic, much to her parents' displeasure. She had become more and more drawn to his religion and not only had she been baptized into it but she had decided to become a nun, leaving the grieving boyfriend and probably even more chagrined parents behind! Meeting him was certainly a turning point in her life.

A new career

Another turning point for me came from meeting a masseur who worked with a pendulum for diagnosing. Not knowing or believing in anything of the sort, all I knew in advance was that he could help with a painful hip. I was therefore amazed when, with a mixture of homeopathy and massage, the pain disappeared. This got me fired up to do something similar. Not massage, but reflexology. In a perfect example of synchronicity, a brand-new office colleague had just qualified through a local school and I found my course.

Reading a little complementary medicine magazine afterwards changed my life again. In it was an article with a photo of ear treatment candles. On the very same day a girl who had done her reflexology diploma with me and who lived quite a long way away called me for some information and I mentioned it to her. Would you believe that she had used the candles for several years and swore by them? My colleague, intrigued, obtained a stock and we worked on everyone we could find. Leaving Geneva for London in 1989, I eventually launched them on the UK market in 1991. But of course that's another story which again completely altered the course of my life.

It makes life itself exciting, too, because in all the years we have ahead of us we are bound to meet up with all sorts of occasions which can change our lives in the blink of an eye. Sometimes we're confronted with a crossroads and there our lives can go along in the same way if we take one road, but if we take another all sorts of things could happen.

Making decisions

James Redfield in *The Celestine Prophecy* tells of a moment when the narrator is confronted with just such a situation. Arriving where two roads forked, both of which would have taken him to his destination, he stopped and tried to relax. He focused on first one and then the other until suddenly, beside one of the roads, he noticed a carpet of little white flowers and as he looked they began to glow, so this was the one he chose. He hadn't gone very far when he was arrested by the forces who were trying to destroy the ancient manuscript, the search for which forms the subject of the book. Cursing to himself that he had taken the wrong road, he was thrown into a jail cell with a young man who was able to give him a vital piece of information he had been seeking and he realized that he *had* done the right thing—it just hadn't seemed like it at the time: a life-changing event that at first glance appeared to be negative. Had he chosen the other road he would have probably ended up as a prisoner anyway at some point but without the information he needed to protect himself and to move on.

When something unexpected, good, bad or tragic enters our lives, it could be the moment that opens up a whole new vista and our destiny takes a dramatically different route. What is quite stunning is that each morning when we wake up and go over the activities planned for the day we cannot possibly know that by the time we go to bed our whole world could have changed. Forever. Exciting or scary?

Giving Back

'If when I die I've given back more in life than I've taken, then I will have lived a good life.'

The parting words of one of my friends as we left the restaurant after a long and chatty lunch. He and his wife work in Congo and we were having a conversation about the place of Europeans in Africa and what could be done to make the divide between our peoples seem less deep.

His philosophy sounds like a good road map, wherever we may live, and if we never leave our home town it is still something we can take to heart.

We hear so much about the arrogance of people from the West and the plundering and exploitation that has been going on and is still going on in all parts of the developing world: taking from the poorest people on earth, lying to them, using them, just to make us richer. And what have we gained? A higher living standard? Yes, definitely, but a happier one? That is far less sure.

People are amazing

One shining example of a European in Africa is Albert Schweitzer, the doctor from Alsace, who opened his clinic in Lambaréné in Gabon in the 1950s. His extraordinary legacy is being continued in part by a Swiss organization headed by Willy Randin, who, as well as representing the Red Cross in various trouble spots, was appointed to the post of director of Schweitzer's hospital on the death of its founder in 1965. After his years there, where he carried on developing its services, he set up a small non-governmental organization and I have met him at various exhibitions where he has taken a stand to sell products from Africa and Asia and some of the books he has written about his experiences. The last time I saw him he had just come back from a trip to Gabon and his first comment to me was that when he read news about Africa in the

West, the media seemed to be talking about a different planet.

During his stay at Lambaréné he was able to arrange for Swiss doctors and dentists to train local people and now his organization offers possibilities for retired people and teenagers to go out for a couple of weeks at a time and work side by side with the locals, constructing and repairing. For some of the young people it has been a life-changing experience and has sent them in a completely different direction in life from the one they had planned. Many local villages in his home corner of Switzerland have joined in the effort and now hold events to raise money to be used in Lambaréné to finance the improvements which are continually being made. As Mr Randin is advancing in years, his son Philippe, who shares his vision, is working with him.

You and me

But, you know, it isn't only people like my friend in Congo, Albert Schweitzer or Willy Randin who are giving back more than they take; it is the many, many other unsung heroes and heroines in every corner of the world. My mother's first, brief marriage was to a man from a hard-working but poor family. She often talked about her then sister-in-law, Dorothy, who would arrive home on Friday evening with the remains of her wages to hand over to her mother and receive a reproach for giving so much of it to beggars on the way home.

'Oh Mum, he was *such* a poor old man' was her invariable comment; London in those days was full of genuine hardship.

Dorothy wasn't doing it to gain brownie points; in fact she was quite embarrassed at not giving her mother all her wages. The little she had she was prepared to share with those who didn't have anything at all and what is so wonderful is that she is just one of hundreds of thousands of people who every day are finding ways, without any fanfare, in which to give back more than they take. It's what makes the world a good place to be and it gives us hope for the future.

Less Is More

E.F. Schumacher was an economist with a difference and his view of the art of living was always to make a good thing out of a bad thing. Although classically trained with John Maynard Keynes he became less and less orthodox in his views and in 1973 he brought out a very important work entitled *Small Is Beautiful: Economics As If People Mattered*. He wrote other collections of essays and was credited with taking up Mahatma Gandhi's ideas on appropriate technology, which is now also referred to as 'sustainable development'. *Earth supplies enough to satisfy every man's need but not every man's greed*, was Gandhi's view.

Schumacher echoed his views, insisting that the world provides everything mankind really needs in the way of living space, food, adequate shelter and materials to build essentials; we know enough about ecology to keep our planet in good shape, too. So why don't we take this on board?

Many of us do, but we know in our hearts that 'growth' is an absolute buzzword to all governments who need to insist that their economies are healthy because they're growing. Nothing could be more wrong or more destructive in the long run. The only way to save our planet is to achieve minus growth. Of course millions of producers of life's frills would go out of business, although if we really took Schumacher's eminently sensible ideas seriously, masses of jobs could be created in green industries. We could also learn more about sharing—although for those still wedded to the idea that more is better, a whole new way of looking at our world could be terrifying.

What we can do

Some of us endeavor to become thoughtful consumers. Not buying more than we need and passing on to someone else anything we no longer use. Not taking plastic bags at the supermarket, we try to ensure that our purchases are from sustainable sources and not made in foreign sweat shops and we seek out Fair Trade products. These may cost a bit more—and that's by no means always the case—although not only will we be getting better quality, we'll be improving the lives of those who are making them.

We think about car pools where we can have the use of a car only when we need it. Going into the town center at any time of day and seeing all the cars rushing past, I can't help noticing that 90 per cent have only one person in them. We need to think about mobile phones, whose use not only doesn't do our health any favors, and that has now been proved, but helps to destroy the ozone layer with the masts which are being erected everywhere. Listen to any conversation, and it's almost impossible to take a bus or train or sit in a bar or restaurant without overhearing someone speaking much too loudly into a mobile, and you could say that 90 per cent of those calls aren't really necessary either.

When the latest computer game or the newest electronic gadget comes out, people queue for hours to get their hands on it. They've possibly already got a cupboard full of the things at home but they're not the very latest model that has been advertised widely or that they've seen in the hands of one of the famous-for-five-minutes pseudo-celebrities.

I have read that the energy used by appliances on standby throughout the world would be enough to power one reasonably sized city. It beats me that when people leave work for the evening, the weekend or even to go on a trip many of them have actually left their computers switched on. So logging on in the morning would take a few minutes more. Well, we're never *that* rushed.

The critical mass

A journalist in a Sunday newspaper nearly ten years ago was commenting on the world and where we're headed and his parting shot was that change rarely comes from one particular event. It comes from the effect of millions of tiny invisible changes, impalpable personal micro-decisions, which one day attain a critical mass and that's what torpedoes the obsolete to make way for the new.

Many people have understood and are doing their bit for the planet but at the moment there are still too many interests involved in having more and if it means that people go without life's necessities such as clean water, adequate food or a roof over their heads then we should see how we can change things. And we can change things, every single one of us; we can change things because when we work to light the path for others, we light our own path. We hold the solution.

People Who Touch Our Lives

Do you sometimes suddenly think of someone you haven't seen for years? Or someone whom you met just briefly ages ago? Does it make you wonder why you're suddenly thinking about them after such a long period or after one short meeting? When that happens to me I certainly feel there's a reason and that they have a message of some sort. If a friend with whom I've lost touch or even an acquaintance from the past who briefly crossed my path comes to mind, I mentally send them blessings. I don't know why they have entered my thoughts, seemingly out of the blue, but perhaps it's just for that reason.

I remember having a dream once about a dancing partner, not even a boyfriend, I had when I was a teenager and to whom I had been really unkind. His life was quite sad because his mother had died when he and his two brothers were very young and although they had been raised by loving grandparents as their father was unable to care for them on his own, of course it wasn't the same. Keith appeared in a vivid dream many, many years later and I got very upset at the thought of how nasty I had been, so I mentally asked him to forgive me. He stayed in my thoughts for around a week and then his image vanished so I had probably laid the ghost to rest.

An old school friend
Not so long afterwards a girl who was at school with me came to mind one evening when I was meditating. Jean was a year or so older at a time when age differences mattered to most children, but not to her and we became friendly. She lived in a small village and when we left school we lost touch. I heard later that she had had an affair with the village bad boy, fallen pregnant and been sent to stay with an aunt before giving birth to a baby who was immediately adopted. My informant, a colleague who

lived in the same village, considered it a pointless exercise as everyone was in on what was an open secret. She was able to return to her family after the birth, and when 10 or 15 years later I met a girl who worked with her, she talked about a constant sadness that seemed to cling to Jean.

The last time I saw her was over 20 years ago. I was staying with my mother when I bumped into her on her way to work. I teased her that she was a bit late and she smiled and said she'd stopped to help a girl whose car had broken down. That was typical Jean, always ready to help anyone; in short, a thoroughly decent person. Why did she slip into my thoughts so many years later? No idea, but what I *could* do was mentally to wish her well and hope that she and her son had been reunited.

Those who come to meet us

When reading accounts of near-death experiences I have often been struck by the fact that many people who have had them tell interviewers about being met by former neighbors, their first employer, people who hadn't had much of an impact on their lives, people they had completely forgotten and to whom they never gave a single thought, before being told to go back as it wasn't yet their time. Sometimes the contact in life had been so fleeting and so far in the past that they had no possible conscious memory of that person.

Mitch Alborn wrote a novel entitled *The Five People You Meet in Heaven*. It is about just that: the last moments on earth of an elderly man and the first five people he meets when he dies. Although one of them he didn't even physically meet while alive, they all contributed something to his existence in such a way as to make him into the man he became. He ends up understanding how, by touching his life in some manner, they changed its course, and, finally, what he meant to the world. Of course it's only a novel and it is *extremely* sentimental but it does give food for thought.

The Kindness of Strangers

Puffing hard, I carried on running although I had little hope of catching the bus; on the town's outskirts buses are not very frequent. Well, I didn't make it, glaring after it in frustration and imagining that the 20-minute wait for the next one (and that was a best-case scenario) was the end of the world. We, or rather I, often do think like that, when 20 minutes out of a life is less than nothing and quickly forgotten.

As I stood there, hands on hips, a car stopped and a lady opened the passenger door.

'Jump in,' she urged, 'we'll catch it down the road.'

Which we did, very easily.

I don't know if the driver had done that sort of thing before but had I been in her place my reflexes certainly wouldn't have clicked in so fast. Her kindness made missing the bus at my usual stop really worthwhile. For all I knew, she might have been in a hurry to get somewhere and picking me up was delaying her.

Trustworthy people trust others

Another instance of a complete stranger showing kindness was when I had just started to live in Switzerland and, stopping at the supermarket to buy food for supper, I found I'd left my purse in my office drawer. The cashier told me flatly that the only option was to put the items I'd picked up back on the shelves. At that moment an elderly lady leading the queue building up behind me offered to lend me the money to pay.

'Do you know this person?' The cashier looked extremely suspicious.

'No, but she has an English accent and I trust English people,' came the reply.

Obviously considering her a fool, the cashier took her money and I took her address, passing by the next evening after work with the money and some flowers to thank her. She wasn't in the least surprised to see me because she'd believed I'd pay her back. It wasn't a huge sum and had I not paid her she wouldn't have been in financial difficulties but it was such a wonderful gesture on her part and, again, I don't know if I'd have been sufficiently quick to do the same. Instead I'd probably have been standing there fuming about someone holding me up!

The good Samaritan

What was probably the most amazing piece of unsolicited kindness from a stranger I have ever experienced up to now happened when I was very young and living in Scotland. My boyfriend and I had been to a party and had had a row when we got back to my home. He left me in floods of tears and as I lived on a main road, I decided to walk up and down as sleep was out of the question. I hadn't gone far when a car driven by a young man seemingly a few years older than me stopped and he wound down his car window. I have often wondered since how someone driving along a wide, empty main road had been able to notice a pedestrian in tears.

'Can I help; you seem to be in trouble?' he enquired.

'No, just leave me alone, I'm fine,' I replied, although this was patently untrue.

'Look, why don't you tell me about it? We can get a coffee at the machine down the road and then we can drive round a bit and at least you won't be walking the streets in the middle of the night for the police to pick you up and cause problems.'

There he made me pause because the Glasgow police force had a fearsome reputation in those days and it was always better to avoid having anything to do with them. That immediately swung the balance in favor of his offer.

I got into his car and we stopped at the end of the road where there was a coffee machine. He then drove through Glasgow and out into the country while I must have bored him to tears with my juvenile saga of unrequited love. After an hour or two he dropped me off at home. Gathering my wits I thanked him and asked him why he had been so kind. He explained that he had a sister my age and if she were ever in the same state he would like to feel that someone had taken care of her. I don't think we even exchanged names and our paths never crossed again. But what an amazing person.

When I told my boyfriend's mother (certainly not daring to tell my own) about it ages afterwards she was aghast. Angry with her son for leaving me in such a state, she was horrified that I'd got into a car with a perfect stranger. She was quite right of course and I don't know whether it was because I was past caring or because he had an aura about him that made me feel safe. There was definitely someone looking out for me that night, that's for sure.

The Tekos School and *The Ringing Cedars of Russia*

It was very uplifting to read an article about the Green School in Indonesia and to know that from small beginnings amazing things are happening everywhere, offering children a new way of relating to the world and a new method of learning, raising their consciousness and equipping them for a very different future. When we leave the mainstream press behind, we come across all sorts of gems like this, proving that the world is not always the way it may seem.

I want to tell you about another school, quite different from the Green School and totally different from any other school in the world, but first I need to paint in the background, so bear with me.

Anastasia's world

You may not have heard of *The Ringing Cedars of Russia*, which is a set of nine books relating the meetings between Anastasia, a real person (Man, as she refers to herself) and a Russian trader named Vladimir Megré who 'coincidentally' came across her deep in the Siberian pine forests on one of his business trips. She told him he would write a book that would be read all over the world and he would become a rich man. Megré's life was completely changed by this experience and, as he recounts in Book 2, he went to Moscow with the idea of setting up an ethical business network. All his efforts turned to dust, and having lost his business, his money and his family, he tells of how he lived on the street in Moscow until he obeyed Anastasia's plan—he wrote a book. Help came immediately in the form of three students who paid his rent on a small apartment and uploaded his work free of charge onto a computer; a small printing house which did the first print-run free and whose books sold out in record time; and that wonderful publicity machine, 'word of mouth'.

To date the books have been translated into 20 languages and read by over 10 million people. Not bad for a self-published set! Why self-published? Well, Megré wanted to ensure that the story stayed *his* story and was not changed to make it more commercially successful by a big publishing house, which is very ethical of him because it is difficult to find any information about the books outside Russia. Although this is a series, the first book has changed the lives of hundreds of thousands of people in Russia alone and deserves to reach the widest public possible because *this* has to be our future, the way we need to go and the way that many people in Russia are already going.

That, however, is not the story I want to tell.

A well-kept secret

Anastasia, the extraordinary woman Vladimir Megré met, gave him a vision of a totally new kind of school which sounded so wonderful he didn't believe it could exist. But it did and it does. It is the Tekos School in southern Russia and its director is a visionary and poet, academician Mikhail Petrovich Shchetinin. In this school, which has been built and decorated by the children themselves, the normal rules have been turned upside down and they learn from and teach one another. The age range is from 8 to 17; they get through a ten-year curriculum in a couple of years and can obtain a recognized academic degree by the age of 15–17. They study many subjects, such as serving their country (which does *not* include fighting in wars), ethics, preservation of folk traditions, languages, architecture, etc. Education is free and when Book 3, which describes the school in detail, was published a few years ago there was already a waiting list of 2500 children. The students cook their own meals, write their own textbooks; they dance, draw and sing. The remarkable thing is that this school has been in existence for 30 years, mysteriously burning down a few years ago, only to be rebuilt by the children themselves. In all those years of its existence most of us have never even heard of it!

People from other countries are starting to become interested and, as with the Green School, the Steiner schools want to become involved in bringing the concept to a much wider public and, more importantly, giving an opportunity to a growing number of children to start life more holistically. It sounds like an excellent blueprint for the future.

The Wonders of Our World

Some years ago I was in the Jura Mountains in Switzerland working as a monitor at a summer camp for children from 12 to 14 years old. The only evening diversion my fellow workers and I had once the children were in bed was to cross the fields by the light of the moon and unwind with a few beers down in the village. One evening as we crossed the meadows I looked up at the sky and was absolutely and utterly awestruck by the magnificent light show above me.

'What's that?' I managed to splutter.

Twenty-year-old Chris looked up and remarked casually: 'Oh, that's the Milky Way.'

I had never seen anything like it; I've never seen it since and it was totally unforgettable.

We only have to look

Many people take holidays to exotic places and come back full of the wonders they have seen. I haven't traveled much, but an afternoon spent in silent company with a friend in the sand dunes of Morocco is one of my memories. Another is sailing down the Nile on a felucca from Aswan to Luxor, slipping along in rhythm with the life on its banks. I've seen some breathtaking landscapes in the North American national parks, but I don't feel we have to travel long distances to see some of the world's wonders because they are on every continent and in every country.

For example, one Whit Monday in May, I was hiking in the mountains with a friend when we topped a rise and suddenly came across a huge dip filled with hundreds and hundreds of jonquils in full bloom.

Because I come from London I find the parks and squares with their profusion of daffodils in spring a delight, as are the bluebell woods further out in the country; that is, those that have not yet disappeared. The red and white blossoms on the chestnut trees brighten up our city streets and even in the autumn, with their leaves turning bronze; their very shape makes them things of beauty. Trees are a particular love of mine, and mature beeches and oaks, to say nothing of sequoias, seem so majestic. We had a huge weeping willow in the communal garden of our apartment block in London and it was wonderful to sit under it in the heat of the summer.

Beauty is everywhere

One year, following the itineraries in a book entitled *Guide to the London Country Way*, walking the public footpaths, going through fields and woods and over ridges, my then partner and I navigated the 205-mile route that encircles London. We stayed at youth hostels and the Sunday morning in autumn when we started out early with the sun's rays slanting through the trees in the depths of Epping Forest with nobody else about was a wonderful moment. There we were on the outskirts of a huge city but we could have been deep in the country.

A few years later, living in a part of town not noted for its charm, going out early on a Sunday when most of the world was still asleep and there was hardly any traffic, you could hear the birds singing their hearts out and it really did make me realize that London is a collection of villages and just round any corner from a dreary and noisy main road you are among picturesque small houses with roses in the gardens.

Not only in the natural world

We go off and marvel at exotic landscapes like deserts and mountains because we don't see them at home, but we have unique sights too. Visitors to Britain enjoy the rolling hillsides and the gentle landscape which we take for granted. Beauty is truly in the eye of the beholder. Even man-made beauties such as a Nash terrace are unique and a well-known travel writer has described the revamped St Pancras Station in London, which is now home to the Eurostar terminal and the gateway to the continent, as the world's most wonderful railway station.

These are just some of the things that inspire me in the world in which I live, but wherever we have our home we can find sights in nature to delight us and make us dream; our world is absolutely chock full of beauty and we often fail to appreciate, even to notice its uniqueness, especially when we see it every day. We always seem to want to go ever further afield to find what we consider more beautiful or more exotic, but after hassles and delays at airports, mislaid luggage, a temperature too high or too low, accommodation lacking in comfort, jet lag and perhaps a dose of travelers' tummy, we can start to appreciate what we have in our own backyards.

We're Pretty OK

Clearing out a drawer one day I came across a photocopy of a newspaper cutting I'd saved from years before. I can't quote it chapter and verse but can just pick out some of the ideas that really appealed to me.

When our car is stuck in a traffic jam, do we ever give a thought to people to whom the idea of owning a car is something to which they can never aspire?

When work is getting us down, do we think about people desperately searching for a job just to put food on the table?

When our car breaks down and we have to hike to the nearest garage, do we think about the handicapped person forced to sit and wait to be rescued, who would love to be able to walk somewhere, anywhere?

When we look in horror at our first grey hair, do we think about people who for one reason or another have lost all their hair and would love to see one of any color growing on their heads?

What can we learn from that?

Well, the thought behind all that is that there's always someone far worse off than we are; in fact far, far worse off. Now I'm not going to cast aside the idea that those of us whose basic needs are met are immune to tragedy, despair and hopelessness. For instance, I remember when I was very young and was worrying about what to give my boyfriend for Christmas. In November he unexpectedly told me it was over. I wept buckets of tears on the shoulders of anyone who would listen, and when a good friend said that at least I didn't have to worry about his present anymore, I realized that if he had phoned to tell me he still wanted to be with me, I would gladly have gone shopping for it.

Often we don't appreciate something that is working until it stops, and it is quite a good idea to be thankful for what we have rather than concentrating on what we don't have. Of course I'm not the first to think up such a revolutionary notion. But I have noticed that it has been a bit of a theme in my life when I have yearned for something that, even if it wouldn't make my happiness complete, at least would give me a boost. Not only have I found that it is a lot less exciting when it does turn up, but what is worse is that when my wishes have become reality months or even years later, I've gone on to other things and in fact they can prove an obstacle, preventing me from getting what I really want at that moment. For example, when my first book was published in 2003 a friend said, and I believed her too, that my life would really take off. Well, it didn't and I was *so* disappointed.

Moving on

It is certainly a measure of our progress in life in that we've got further than we thought when our fondest dreams of a few years ago no longer enchant us and we realize that we've moved on. Reaching for something is important, and on the wall above my computer I have a star carved in wood by a friend. I love it because to me it proves that I can reach for the stars, all the while trying to bear in mind Theodore Roosevelt's wise saying that it's important to keep our eyes on the stars but to keep our feet firmly on the ground.

SECTION 2: Positive Mindset

Aging or Sageing?

Deepak Chopra in his excellent book *Ageless Aging, Timeless Mind* mentions three factors which in his opinion are vital for staying young at heart. The first is to keep our body weight around the same (give or take a pound or three) for all our adult lives; the second is not to have constant recourse to doctors and medication; and the third is never to retire.

Now by never retiring he certainly doesn't mean we should all be forced to work until we drop. Study after study has postulated that people enjoy being active and useful and that the majority, once they have officially retired, either carry on or go back to work, not because they especially need the money but because they cannot understand why one day they are useful members of staff and the next considered too old; surely nothing can have changed overnight. Some go into self-employment; some even take up careers that they would have liked to have followed earlier; and others decide to study, which they were perhaps unable to do in their youth.

Leave it to the young?

A work colleague in her late thirties used to say very frequently that older employees should move aside and leave jobs for the young people who are starting out in life. Well, OK, cards on the table, I am in the former category but it's still a spurious argument; when I told her my father died the same weekend he retired, as she started to say 'What a shame that was' I quickly added that he was 78 and it was probably the idea of stopping work that had carried him off!

A certain amount of experience is a distinct plus in a job and whether you've been a dabbler in all sorts of fields or whether

43

you have stayed honing your knowledge and skills in just one area, you have something precious to contribute. Also the fun of late nights and wild parties tends to have worn off and you are less likely to take time off from work to recover.

Voluntary Service Overseas (VSO) has a policy of engaging mature people with a lifetime's experience of teaching rather than someone fresh out of college, especially if they are working with a practical trade such as mechanics or motor maintenance in which they have probably worked for several decades. Having been in contact with all types of people, they often have good communication skills too.

The policy of a major DIY chain in the UK is to hire older people, which seems fairly logical. I mean, if you're going to do some home decorating for the first time, would you rather ask the advice of an enthusiastic 20-year-old or an experienced 60-year-old who has probably done a fair bit of it in his or her time?

Where older people have triumphed

I once listened to a program about men working on cruise ships. Many of the passengers going on cruises are single elderly women, often widows, and in the evenings there are far too few men for them to dance with. One cruise line had a novel idea and that was to recruit older men as dancing partners. The men they hired, also all single elderly men who could dance, on finding themselves alone in life, had taken up a whole new career sailing the world's oceans in five-star comfort, their only job being to dance with the spare ladies and maybe to accompany groups on outings. Sounds like a great career option.

Here's another true story I found that illustrates the role of older people in the workplace perfectly. It was about Tom Hopperton, a man of 69 who was working as a skater in his local Tesco supermarket. His job was to skate off and fetch an item a shopper arriving at the check-out had forgotten and he estimated that he covered around five miles a day. He explained that, when he saw the job advertised, he decided to apply in person because the people hiring would never have believed he was capable of doing it if he'd just telephoned. He is very likely to have been right about that.

Be Careful What You Wish For

Volumes have been written about the Law of Attraction which teaches us how to attract what we want in life, although many people have missed the real meaning or have not bothered to look deeper. It's a law that's completely impartial and it doesn't care one way or the other about what we attract, which means that if we're of a negative mindset we can draw into our lives all sorts of unwanted people and situations. In our euphoria in learning how to get what we want from life, we tend to forget that aspect.

The Law of Attraction works because everything is energy. How many people do we know who seem to lead charmed lives? Whose glass is always half full and never half empty? Who always seem to get what they want from life? Not only do they have a positive outlook but they believe that whatever they are looking for is looking for them: their energy level is latching on to a compatible one elsewhere.

Children understand the concept

I remember reading a modern parable about a small boy who believed that things would always turn out the way he wanted. When he asked for a horse for his birthday his father decided to test him. He had a load of horse manure delivered to the backyard. When the little boy woke up the next morning and saw it he went into raptures: 'Great, thank you, Daddy—where have you hidden the horse?'

The tale finishes there and I don't think it's even a true one but I'm positive that in real life the boy would have got his horse because he didn't harbor any doubts in the matter.

Children are much easier to work with because they have no problems with attracting good outcomes; they *believe*, that is until well-meaning parents and teachers, wanting to protect them from disappointment, knock the optimism out of them.

I am reminded of another story, true this time, which I read in a magazine a few years ago.

Avril, a 10-year-old girl in the USA, saw a coloring competition advertised by a local shop and she not only decided to enter, but planned to win a prize. Her parents and sisters tried to tell her that there would be lots of children entering and she might not win anything. She was adamant and immediately started to do the prettiest picture she could. It was submitted and there was no news for a while. Her family continued to tell her that she would probably not be one of the lucky ones but it had no effect on her at all: she was going to win. One morning the postman arrived with a huge box. In it was a beautiful doll for Avril who had won the top prize in her age group. She was delighted, but to her mother's amazement, not in the least surprised; she had expected to win.

Jonny Wilkinson, the England rugby player who has now retired, was always certain he was going to be a winner. His mother tells of how at the age of 4, he used to line up toilet rolls on the lounge floor and kick them over imaginary goalposts. The reason he gave was that if he needed to take a kick to win a match for England one day he wouldn't need to worry about doing it. Amazing sentiments for a small boy, although his prophecy did come true when 20 years later, in the dying minutes of the last game, he won the rugby World Cup for England. What a thriller that was.

A note of caution

Now let's look at the other side of the Law of Attraction when we draw to us something we don't want at all. In her book *You Can Heal Your Life* Louise Hay tells the story of one of her students who won 500 dollars. He was over the moon: he repeated over and over again how unbelievable it was because he had never ever won anything.

What happened next was that he had an accident and had to pay out 500 dollars in medical bills. He didn't believe his luck, so the energy dissipated and his winnings disappeared back into the ethers.

Louise also talks about blessing our bills as the energy they come from knows we have the money to pay them, and I surprised the postman one morning when he was about to deliver a letter for me.

'It's only a bill,' he explained apologetically.

Not missing a beat, I came right back with: 'Oh great—only rich people receive bills.'

He stared at me open-mouthed! It's a fact that when we feel rich we give bigger tips, perhaps buy a few flowers or a surprise gift for someone, or order a more expensive dish in a restaurant. When we feel poor, we make do with any old thing and try to see how we can economize and what we can manage without. This is how the Law of Attraction works. If we feel poor and act poor, we are putting out the message that we *are* poor, that we have little and don't expect life to improve. When we give (and that includes giving to ourselves), knowing the fund is inexhaustible, we are bringing prosperity into our belief system and we will automatically attract more. That is universal law.

The power of words

It has been said that we should be careful what we wish for because we might get it. We also need to watch our language. When I read Louise Hay's book over 20 years ago I realized that I was in the habit of using the word 'unbelievable' far too frequently. When meeting someone who asked me how I was, the answer was likely to have been 'Not bad'. These words have been banished from my vocabulary in that context; and I'd really like to know who thought up the expression 'to die for'? Nothing is worth dying for when it's applied to a pair of expensive shoes or a particularly delicious cake.

So whatever our thoughts, if we want to have a happy and successful existence, we really must try to look on the bright side. In that way our energy will stay high and we'll only attract good things into our lives.

Everything Speaks to Me

This was the title of a book I bought a few years ago, and as I can't remember the name of the author and nothing comes up on the web, it must have dropped off the radar. Which is a pity because we would do well to take its title to heart and absorb the author's examples of how paying attention to her intuition helped her to develop a more discerning eye and ear.

Anything, whether a book or a remark someone makes or a thought that slips through our minds like a bird flying past, could contain an important message for us and most of the time we don't even register it. We read the book, reply to the remark, hardly notice the thought and go on our way.

Living mindfully

The Buddhists have an expression for it: they call it 'living mindfully', and that is an excellent way to look at life. It doesn't mean getting paranoid, and, as certain things have different meanings for different people, it pays to take note of our gut feelings each time.

For example, in the UK, a black cat is considered lucky and if one crosses a bride's path on her wedding day then that is the ultimate in good luck, although in many other countries, a black cat is considered to be very unlucky.

Similarly a crow. For the shamanic peoples the crow or the raven represents justice—just think of the black gowns that are worn by lawyers in court. I have read that the eye of the crow is the gateway into other worlds, although for certain cultures they are birds that portend a death. Interestingly the sight of a blackbird which comes from the same family as the crow, as it sings its beautiful song to announce the arrival of summer, is universally welcomed.

Listening to our intuition

In a completely different way of taking heed of the signs, a couple of friends of mine were house hunting and arrived at one that looked really good from the outside. The lady, a very psychic person, immediately started to feel something oppressive as she walked around the ground floor and decided not to go any further. Her husband, who had gone upstairs and who usually scoffed at her ideas, came down at a run and as they walked outside, gave her a sidelong look, remarking: 'You felt it too, didn't you?'

When it comes to other people, it's not a bad thing to look at who our friends are and why we like them. That way we get a more accurate picture of ourselves and who *we* are. If everyone we meet is unreliable, what is that saying about us? It's important to know.

Do you sometimes have the feeling that something isn't quite right about a situation? That someone everyone else seems to like doesn't quite ring true with you? It's in our interest not to ignore the messages we're getting, although others may tell us we're being silly or imagining things. Remember Miss Marple in the Agatha Christie detective novels? She always got her man (or woman) because she picked up the little hints, the memory joggers, the vague resemblance to another person she had known who had turned out to be sly or untrustworthy. We, too, would do well to listen more to our gut feelings. Our impressions may be dismissed as stupid by others but if we stick to what we feel, we could save ourselves from a painful situation or a deep disappointment later on.

Fear = False Expectation Appearing Real

Quite a few years ago, Gerald Jampolsky wrote a book called *Love Is Letting Go of Fear*. He postulated that love and fear were opposites, when I had always thought that hate was the opposite of love. But when hate is boiled down and examined, it often turns into a fear of something or someone outside our present level of experience.

If we take these two emotions as the two extreme ends of the spectrum then life becomes easier to understand because we know what we love; we know because we've done it or tried it or lived it. Fear, on the other hand, is all about something we don't know but imagine will be awful, although experience ought to teach us that we rarely need to fear the unknown and it might even turn out to be great.

I first came across Jampolsky's book at a workshop where the speaker insisted that the initials F-E-A-R stand for False Expectation Appearing Real. And that's what fear is. It's always related to something in the future, even the immediate future like being at the top of an icy ski slope, about to hurtle down it. We may be terrified that it will be dangerous; we could fall and hurt ourselves badly. It's because we're in unknown territory. We don't feel any fear if we've done it successfully before; we expect the experience to be totally exhilarating.

Going past fear

Isn't it great when we've been terrified of doing something, often for the first time, and have found it to work out better than we thought? When I had to stand up in front of a class of 20-odd students who were expecting me to teach them English I was absolutely terrified. I don't remember that first evening much, but as time went on it became easier. Now, after several years, I enjoy going into a new class every October and meeting a whole new group of people.

The first time I had to stand on a stage and give a presentation caused me a few sleepless nights although, happily, I had a microphone to hold onto which provided a bit of moral support. I'd made a note of the main points and although never really at ease straight away, it is probably better like that—too much confidence could be disastrous. It's said that many actors suffer from nerves and some are physically sick before a performance but that doesn't impair their performance.

When you know things are going well with your talk and the audience is with you, it spurs you on to greater efforts; you start moving away from your carefully prepared text as ideas come tumbling into your mind and, at the end when you're receiving the applause you know you deserve, it is a magnificent feeling. You've overcome the fear.

Belief in ourselves

Susan Jeffers wrote a book called *Feel the Fear and Do It Anyway*. Well, we must work through it. Even if it's not about something you absolutely need to do, when you have faced the fear down and overcome it, you *do* feel better, although like climbing a range of hills, there's always another challenge up in front. Jeffers tells us that when she started teaching people how to improve their lives she always prepared far more class material than she could possibly need. I still keep this tip in mind when giving an English lesson although, with experience, I can usually manage to keep the students occupied if we get through the work faster than I'd expected. The initial fear of standing in front of the class or not being able to teach them what they need to learn has been well and truly overcome.

I'd love to be one of those people who sail through life not seeming to have a fear of anything and always expecting the best to happen to them. And so I could be without any difficulty whatsoever *if* I could just believe it.

Going the Extra Mile

The very first job I applied for was a fishing expedition because I wanted to work in a legal firm and so I sent an unsolicited application to a well-regarded local partnership. The reply was that they had no need of anybody for the moment but blah, blah, blah.

So I wrote back, thanking them very much and saying that as I intended to make the law my career (how many million times has it changed since then?), I hoped they would think of me if they had something suitable in the future. Surprisingly, they replied immediately, invited me for interview and offered me my first job.

That was a massively important lesson: how often do we neglect to follow up an initial refusal because we consider the matter closed? Working as a freelance, I once sent out a load of CVs and quite a few companies replied. Many said they didn't need the services I offered and some that they would contact me if something came up. I e-mailed all of those back, principally to thank them for their replies and reiterating my availability. A friend with whom I once worked always held that you have to put energy into something if you want it to work—in other words, go the extra mile—and I have found this to be very true. If I *know* I have left no stone unturned then I don't have the nagging feeling that if I had done more I'd have had a better result. The extra mile is never busy and a friend who goes cross-country skiing has provided a great analogy. The first café on his route is invariably packed but as he gets further and further along the track he's frequently out on his own.

Networking means everyone wins

When I had a stand at exhibitions in the UK in the 1990s, promoting ear treatment candles and giving demonstrations and treatments, many people who came to make enquiries left with information on something quite different because I kept literature about therapists I could vouch for and the visitor's problem may have called for a different type of specialty. My job was to sell candles but it was also to put out information to help people help themselves and that is still my aim when giving courses or treatments. Successful people are those who go the extra mile for everyone, not just themselves or their clients, putting people in touch with someone who may be able to offer something more suited to their needs; networkers, in fact.

A matter of respect?

Many times I have called someone with a request for information and sat waiting for the phone to ring with the answer. Which doesn't always happen. If that person can't find the information immediately I would really appreciate a call to tell me it was taking longer than s/he had thought. Is it respect? Is respect another way to look at going the extra mile? I suspect in some cases it may be.

A translator who did some work for me once explained being way over the deadline because her son had broken his arm and she was busy with a well-paid full-time contract. When she finally delivered the work, she certainly wasn't kidding! It was a really sloppy job. As a freelance I am well aware of the need to follow up and work until midnight if I have to; personal matters shouldn't come into it; clients who want their work done also deserve that respect.

Being the best

Another way of going the extra mile is ensuring that we are the very best we can be at what we do. Some people are certainly more talented in one direction than another, but we can always work to the best of our ability with the talents we *do* have so as to offer the very highest service, treating a tiny job with the same importance as one that could set us up for life.

From an entirely practical point of view, clients are going to go for the person who offers the best service and will return to the one who has done the most professional job. When people have talked to me about the crisis, I wonder what crisis they mean. If we always do our best, follow up every possible lead, do an honest job, deliver top quality work on time, share any information that could help someone else, express gratitude to anyone who helps us, then we're all winners.

Knowing When to Run

What you fight to get, you fight to keep. I don't know who said it but how many times have we struggled and fought to get something we wanted or to be somewhere we wanted to be only to find that when we get there it isn't what we really wanted at all? How often do we get little signs along the road telling us, nay, shouting at us that we're heading for disaster? Many years ago Marilyn Monroe sang a song called 'After You Get What You Want You Don't Want It' and that puts the situation into perspective.

My own experience happened years ago when I hadn't yet learnt to listen to my intuition. I had worked at a conference in the south of France for three weeks and, always wanting to be somewhere I wasn't, it gave me the idea to buy a small apartment and get a job in Nice. Having worked out my notice and taken my pension fund with me, I had money to burn. Off I went and an agency quickly found me a small studio apartment in a decent area. I paid my deposit and was to return in a month or so to sign the papers and pay the balance.

Itching to get back and start life in the sun, the day I left London I was taking a minicab to Victoria Station for the one boat train of the day—there was no Easyjet in 1990. Well, we got stuck in traffic and I missed the train! The cab driver took me home and I made arrangements to leave the next day. I shared my sleeper with an elderly man who lived on the streets (and he smelled as if he did). A friend had given him a train ticket and he was off to camp in his garden for the winter. Now I would listen to him with much more attention as he definitely had some important things to say.

Pushing at a closed door

Arriving in Nice I found a dreary little hotel as it was November and there was no electricity in my apartment which, when I visited it, seemed deadly dreary too. The neighbors' cat had been in and out as the window had been left open a crack and he had used the place as a toilet. Even though they had cleaned it thoroughly I still didn't fancy staying there, but the winter closure of the hotel forced my hand. So I reluctantly moved in, battling constantly with the guy who was supposed to be doing a few necessary jobs and was always somewhere else. Nothing went right, but I was struggling to make things happen. All the signs pointed to finding a tenant quickly and going back to London but I soldiered on.

As I was still harboring dreams of living in the sunshine, the agency easily talked me into buying another apartment with a loan secured on the rent I would receive from letting the first one and I jumped at the chance. It was only afterwards I realized I had paid way over the odds for both. Finally, getting fed up, frittering money away just on surviving, not finding a job or anyone to rent either apartment, I left them with the agency and went back to London.

A useful insight

The upshot was that the first apartment went unrented for months, the loan could not be repaid and the bank repossessed the lot. Did I lose a minute's sleep over it? Not really, but I did learn two very important lessons. The first was that when we're up against it from all directions and nothing goes smoothly, it's far better just to cut our losses. The second lesson was that whatever happens to us is not the end of the world; indeed it very often contains a valuable piece of information for the future. If we don't understand these two things we can spend the rest of our lives regretting something we did or didn't do and dreaming about how it could have been different. We need to remember that the past is behind us and its gift is to encourage us to do things differently another time.

We don't have to lie on the bed we've made; that's a fallacy because we can always get out and make it again.

Living with Handicaps

Death is probably the most fraught subject in the world. People just don't like thinking about it but it happens to all of us and there's nothing we can do to avoid it. Helping someone to die is another aspect on which people have sharply differing views.

I recently listened to a program about Alison Davis, born with spina bifida and other handicaps. She is constantly on morphine and even that doesn't always alleviate her intractable pain which sometimes makes her pass out with its intensity. She explained how for many years she'd wanted to die and had made several attempts to end her life.

Seeing how others coped

It was during a trip to India in 1995, where she met disabled children whom she had sponsored and whom she began to love very deeply, that she turned to Colin Harte, her appropriately named carer, and told him she wanted to live. This led to their setting up a charity for disabled Indian children which they called Enable.

Alison had met Colin when he was a student who wasn't particularly enjoying his studies at university and who then decided to become her full-time carer despite an extremely negative reaction from his family. He has looked after her for over 20 years, seemingly utterly content to have given up any idea of a different sort of life and devoting himself to Alison and their charity as well as campaigning against euthanasia.

On a more personal level

Some years ago I spent several weeks as a helper at a summer camp for severely disabled children, all suffering from cerebral palsy. The idea was to give the children a holiday but it was really all about giving their parents a break because these children would have been far happier at home with the people they were used to around them. Knowing that complete strangers (most of whom were young and inexperienced) were looking after their precious children meant that even the parents couldn't relax and enjoy the time they had to themselves.

We were each allotted a child to care for and although one or two of the helpers were only 16 or 17, they became so caught up in what they were doing that some decided to make caring their career. When I attended the initial meeting with the parents I was struck by how protective they were towards these children, and I know some people consider that having a handicapped child has been a true gift and has taught them an amazing lesson in love and compassion.

I also remember another scenario; that of a child born with handicaps her parents couldn't accept. The couple, who were expats, put her into a home in their own country on the other side of the world and I got the impression that they were cutting all ties with her. They had another, healthy baby around a year later. In a similar situation, one of the children at our summer camp was born with brain damage, deaf and blind, and her family had left her in an institution where, although she never went home and was not in contact with her family, she was cared for devotedly, even accompanying her carer to stay with her own family when the home closed for Christmas.

The feelings these parents have about their children are just as important as those of people who devote their lives or their professional careers to looking after a child or an adult who is different. They didn't feel able to do that and, had they been forced, their whole family structure could have broken down, or maybe they would have slid into depression. It must have been a heartbreaking decision to make, whatever they decided to do; something that would possibly continue to haunt them for the rest of their lives.

Making a choice

There is much talk of pro-life and pro-choice but that, too, is a decision that only the people involved can take; someone's beliefs can't be imposed on anyone else. It is easy to say that it's the luck of the draw and people should just get on with bringing up a handicapped child, and many do. One of my mother's cousins had a severely handicapped son and I only visited them once. He was then nearly 30 and they had always taken holidays on canal boats or in rented houses to shield them from pitying eyes. When I met them the parents were aging and their only daughter was about to be married. It can't have been easy for her as she was obviously going to inherit the role of carer later on. As we had no experience of people with mental handicaps, we spent a very uncomfortable evening although the family must have lived through that type of situation many times.

Nobody can decide for us

Then let's look at the other end of life and euthanasia. Who can say whether it's right or wrong? Alison Davis tried and failed to end her pain-filled existence and she's firmly against any form of assisted dying, saying the best years of her life have been since she decided to live, but although that may be true for her it isn't necessarily true for someone else.

And what about those who are called upon to assist? I remember a conversation years ago with a young cousin, a churchgoing Christian, as to whether we would feel able to do this and neither of us could come up with an answer. If it were legal would some people be pushed into taking their own lives by unscrupulous relatives or carers? Would there be sufficient safeguards in place? Or would it be a boon for people who are convinced this is what they want and who don't at present have the means to do anything about it?

It's a cliché to say there are two sides to every question but as we are all individuals one size does *not* fit all. I guess it's best to take things as they come and try not to pass judgment on people who have made choices we don't think we could ever make and which we hope we are *never* called upon to make. Because until we are confronted with a particular situation, we just don't know how we would react.

Raising Our Spirits

A history of art student asked me to proofread her memoir on a specific aspect of art and literature. Not only was it fascinating, not only did it cover a school of painting and poetry about which I knew nothing, but the beauty of the language raised my spirits in such a way that I was almost sorry to deliver the finished article. It had the same uplifting effect as a new ballet that I saw in the same week with its choreography based on the music of Handel.

How good we feel when the sky is bright and the sun shines. That's when it's easy to be happy. When we receive a piece of good news we hadn't been expecting or a compliment or a message out of the blue; when we've enjoyed an excellent meal, when we've met an old friend in town and had a long chat over a drink; all this makes us feel good and raises our spirits.

When things aren't so easy

Let's move on to a time when the rain is beating against the windows, the wind is blowing a gale outside or the snow is falling; when we've had a metaphorical slap in the face from life; when something we had excitedly been looking forward to has been cancelled or turned out to be a lot less fun than expected. What can we do to stay positive? That's when we need to have certain inner resources to tide us over, to raise our spirits until things improve, as of course they will.

We all have different recipes for this. Some people pore over travel catalogues, some pick up an inspiring book or listen to an uplifting piece of music; some tuck into comfort food, some shop until they drop; some take to their beds. Some even sit down and write about it!

Whatever it is, practice makes perfect. Having spent 20 years on self-development, I know there are still moments when beliefs wobble and it is challenging to say the least to stay upbeat. Like any discipline, although it takes work, the benefits are immeasurable.

Keeping the faith

Is there a recipe? Not really, because we're all at different stages in our evolution and have different ideas, but one thing to bear in mind is that we tend to get what we expect out of life so it does pay not to let ourselves sink down so far that it makes getting back up a titanic struggle.

We can only ever see a fraction of the whole picture; it's rather like taking off from an airport in awful weather; rain and low cloud. After some very unpleasant turbulence and what seems an age, although it's usually only a few minutes, the plane breaks through the cloud barrier and into bright sunlight and blue skies and steadies itself. The seat belt lights go off and we settle back to enjoy the journey. Stuck in the murk, we know we'll soon get above it and that it won't take long at all, but it's difficult to imagine when we're bouncing around like peas boiling in a pan on the stove. We have a reference for it because this has happened before so we are aware of the fact that, although very uncomfortable, it's only temporary. When we're stuck in a different kind of murk caused by a problem we think is insurmountable, we can't imagine that just outside our range of comprehension all is well and that's where we're heading.

If we can hold the vision, whether it's about getting to the end of a challenging day or a rough patch in our lives, or even bucketing around in a plane just before soaring up through the clouds to the bright blue skies above, there's always hope. *Hope springs eternal in the human breast*, wrote Alexander Pope and, as Greek mythology tells us, once all the evil had been emptied out of Pandora's Box, hope was the one thing that was left for humanity.

Synchronicity

According to my dictionary, synchronicity is the simultaneous occurrence of two events which appear significantly related but which have no discernible causal connection. We also often use the word 'coincidence' when two events that have little connection with each other happen at the same time—a co-incidence in fact.

As is well known, the concept of synchronicity came from Carl Gustav Jung, the famous Swiss psychiatrist, and the idea has now become quite mainstream. Jung started to research synchronicity as a result of a consultation with a young woman who was recounting a dream she had had of a golden scarab. As she spoke, Jung heard a tapping at the window and, turning round, saw that it was a scarab beetle, the nearest thing to a golden scarab in his part of the world. He had been making little headway with his patient, but after that incident he had a break-through and her therapy took a different route.

It happens all the time

We can find many day-to-day examples of synchronicity: for instance when we think or dream of people we haven't seen for a while and they suddenly turn up in our lives. I once went to buy a birthday card for a friend—a fanatical Queen fan. What should be playing in the card shop but Freddie Mercury singing 'We Are the Champions'.

A mother, waiting for a bus with her child, got into conver-sation with another woman who happened to be a nurse. The mother mentioned that her son had a rash on his body, he was lethargic and she didn't know what was wrong with him. The nurse took one look at the spots, applied a simple test on them and told the mother to get to the nearest hospital as fast as possible. It was meningitis and without her timely intervention the child would likely have died.

Going through a period when work seemed to have dried up completely I began to feel rather bored waiting for something to happen (to say nothing of the financial aspect) as nobody I know is self-employed and during the week they were all happily at their jobs. I mentioned the situation to one of my friends and later that same day he was chatting to a colleague who also knows me. He told her about my search for work and she 'just happened' to mention it to one of her own staff. Her colleague's wife works in a company that 'just happened' to be in desperate need of help and within a few days I had landed a lucrative contract.

I'm sure we all have similar experiences much of the time and we don't always recognize them for what they are because our minds are usually on far more mundane things.

Another example of how it worked for me is this: I was walking to a meeting one evening and for some reason I'd left it far too late to be there for the start. Quickening my pace I mused on the idea of teleporting (a completely different subject where people suddenly find themselves somewhere else and don't understand how they got there). Wouldn't it be wonderful, I thought, if I could be teleported to the door? Smiling at the idea, I plodded on and hadn't gone very far at all when a car pulled up. It was someone attending the same meeting who'd stopped to offer me a lift. A piece of luck, you might say, or a demonstration of synchronicity.

How it worked for others

One lovely story I once read was about a young fashion designer putting the finishing touches to his very first collection. He worked in the same building as a much better-known designer and when an influential buyer arrived to visit the more famous man she got out of the lift at the wrong floor and walked into the young man's showroom. She liked what she saw and bought his entire collection; something he couldn't normally have hoped for in a million years.

Dannion Brinkley survived three near-death experiences and became a best-selling author. After his first experience in 1975, he just could not step telling people about some of the insights he had received until they got absolutely fed up with hearing the same stories and told him to change the record. He became very depressed and began to feel like giving up on life. Then, one day, browsing in his local paper, he found an advertisement for a lecture by Dr Raymond Moody (at that time a young, unknown researcher) on the Near-Death Experience. His heart leapt at finding someone who would understand and make some sense of what had happened to him. At the end of a totally gripping evening where he could relate to everything that was said, he spoke to Moody who, having heard about Brinkley's case, had been trying to find out how to contact *him*. The rest is history as both men have become famous.

Making it work for you

These are just a few instances, but when we look around and live more mindfully we can see all sorts of magical synchronicities and here I make a suggestion. Just for one day or one week take a notebook and write down any seeming coincidences that occur along the way—however tiny they might seem. When we slow down and think about our actions rather than the next item on our list of things to do, we can come across some amazing examples.

The Coming Generation

Much has been written about young people, frequently about how out of control and aimless they are, about their excesses. The number of children being prescribed medication because they are considered to be hyperactive is exploding. The 'what's the world coming to?' reaction is very strong among those who haven't yet looked closely and seen that there is another far more fascinating side to what's going on, where many young people are rejecting the ideas and methods that have served the world for generations and which have contributed to send us crashing into a brick wall. So what is really happening here?

How we are helping

The owner of a bookshop specializing in spiritually based books, in an interview he gave several years ago, said that in his opinion those among us working with the light had raised the planetary vibration, making it easier for children being born to lock onto it and develop their sensitivity at a faster pace. This is why he felt so many so-called indigo and crystal children have arrived among us, and in my dealings with small children and young adults I am constantly amazed by their maturity. Even tiny tots seem to come out with remarks about things that it's taken me a lifetime to learn and which takes their parents' breath away. For example, I have a friend whose 8-year-old daughter writes amazing poetry and her 4-year-old is a philosopher who can give a succinct explanation of what constitutes happiness in a language that 4-year-olds don't usually use.

Their older peers have a view of the world and their place in it which has not the slightest relationship to anything I was thinking at their age. Subjects like the appalling inequality between peoples, ecology and the future of the planet itself have come to the fore in the last 20 years and so many young people are taking up the challenges they pose. They seem to be part of a more thoughtful generation as they assume the banner of the youth revolution which burst onto the scene in the 1960s with the hippies who took the road to Kathmandu and who found a completely different way of living. In fact some of those never came back to the West and a film was made about several who are now of pensionable age and who live very simply in a way we would find challenging but who want nothing else and to whom our materialistic values are an anathema.

Schools offering alternative curricula have sprung up and the Steiner movement in the West has done much to promote the fact that children can learn to be responsible and fulfilled adults in a different way. A friend recently told me these children had problems when they went to university, but then, looking thoughtful, she added that it wasn't a goal for many of them anyway as they consider that so much enforced learning is simply brainwashing.

Putting it into practice

I'm enormously encouraged when I visit the local food market to find a young man who can't be over 30 selling his organic cheeses. His knowledge and passion for what he does are obvious and he's there whatever the weather, advising and explaining. He has expanded his operation and is now helped by his younger brother who also runs a bicycle taxi service. Another stand is managed by a group of people of a similar age who, having obtained qualifications in horticulture, sell fruit, vegetables and home-made sauces and jams from their own organic patch: the peaches and nectarines from their trees have to be tasted to be believed!

Rites of passage

Life for children and young adults used to be much more about having fun and letting responsibility wait, but now from an early age they are exposed to issues they are far too young to cope with. A child psychiatrist once told me what a destabilizing influence giving a child too much choice can be. He (or she) doesn't have the maturity to know what his parents would secretly prefer and that causes him stress. It's easy to imagine, as even for us with the knowledge we have acquired on the way, we are often called upon to make decisions that require a great deal of heart searching.

As a young adult I used to drink industrial quantities of beer; it's part of growing up. Doing things that shock our parents is another rite of passage. But real rites of passage which are still followed in so-called primitive societies are sadly lacking in our world and children can grow up without any sense of identity. In some inner city areas where experiments have been carried out with troubled teenagers, a great deal of excellent work has been achieved, but like all good ideas, funding is never there for something sensible that should be made available to every teenager. It would provide so many benefits to the child and to society, but there are probably vested interests involved so it is unlikely to develop or catch our attention much at the moment, although I'm making no bets on the future.

With a Little Help

A former partner and I were living in a house we shared with other people. The place was invariably crowded and noisy, the TV always on and the back door left open day and night because the cats weren't house-trained and there was no cat flap.

We talked about moving and then my father died suddenly one Christmas Eve. I went to stay with my mother and his funeral took place after Christmas, the day before the snow started falling and falling, sending transport and other links haywire—it became a winter for the record books. A few hours later and the funeral would have been postponed. We were lucky or someone was looking out for us.

When I got back to London, after the peace and order of my mother's home, I just couldn't take the mess and cold any longer. One of the girls had forgotten her keys and, to get in, had had to break a bathroom window which nobody had bothered to repair. To my amazement, my partner said he didn't want to move and, anyway, he didn't think our relationship had a future. Already in an emotional state, it was the last straw.

Time to let go

The following morning, a colleague overhead me telling the tale to a friend and he suggested calling his parents who had two rooms with a shared kitchen and bathroom they rented out: one was vacant. My boss told me to move my things immediately. He booked a parking space for me for the afternoon in the directors' car park and, leaving a note for my now ex-partner, I moved into my new home that evening. Another couple of helping hands making things happen.

The winter was hard and I was desperately unhappy with the loss of my father, my mother's sorrow, a car accident and the breakdown of my relationship, which, although I knew it wasn't going anywhere either, was just too much at once.

Spring came bringing a change of heart and I decided to move further in to the center of town. Not knowing that people hunted for weeks and months for somewhere to live, I bought the weekly paper for the area where I wanted to be to check out the ads at my leisure. This was a paper that had a line of home hunters waiting outside its door on press day to get a copy and start answering ads immediately—the only way to find something decent. Knowing nothing of this, I scanned the ads that evening and found one that sounded just right. I called and went to see it the next day. The two tenants told me they had been inundated with calls and had seen loads of people but had found nobody they really liked. I was offered the spare room on the spot. Again, someone was looking out for me, although at that stage I knew nothing of these things.

Accepting an invitation

Many years later I came back to Geneva to stay with an old friend until I found a job and could rent somewhere to live. It took several weeks but I found a temporary job and then one evening, for some stupid thing I'd done, she let rip; I've rarely seen someone so angry at me. Obviously time to move on. The next day after work I started looking at notice boards in the international organizations and made a couple of phone calls—people didn't use mobiles much at that time so I had to hope that I would find the person at home. One girl gave me an appointment for the next day and I was able to move into her furnished apartment a week later. At the time I called she had just got back home after posting the notice and I was obviously first in line. Luck or something else?

When it was time to move on once again, I quickly found another furnished place but, after a few years, wanted something unfurnished and larger. The rental market at that time was dire and I looked half-heartedly at one or two apartments that had already been let anyway. One Thursday evening I arrived home to find a note from the police pinned to my door. There had been a break-in and they had had the locks changed. The keys were at the local police station.

A helping hand from elsewhere

The next day, having a goodbye lunch with a friend who was leaving that weekend to work abroad, I told him what had happened: 'Why, when I have angels on the front door and an angel inside, would somebody be able to break in?'

He didn't miss a beat: 'They opened the door for you, now move!'

The following Monday I received an e-mail circular from a local letting agency and it just happened that there were two apartments in my area and at my price. I telephoned and, surprise, surprise, was able to visit both of them that evening. I could only apply for one, so, as I had already completed a form, that seemed to be it. Despite a huge number of people applying, within a month it was mine, completely repainted and with brand-new bathroom fittings.

It's now time to move again and I'm hearing the same comments that it's impossible to find anything. When every element is in place, by some amazing feat of synchronicity or a helping hand from somewhere (probably an avenue I had not even thought of exploring), something will happen and I'll be pointed in the right direction.

You Can Do It

It can be very hard to shake ourselves out of the idea that if something has always been done one way, that must be the only way. I can be as bad as the rest, which is crazy because when the habitual way of doing things isn't working then it's time to think out of the box. Much, much easier said than done.

While many of us miss out on all sorts of opportunities, not noticing how beneficial something might have been until it's gone beyond our grasp, others who are more far-sighted are able to snap up any kind of chance that presents itself.

Now that I have been self-employed for several years it is a lot easier to do something new because, to earn a living, that's the only solution. It is more challenging for people who are in a routine job or situation which isn't making them happy but which they are afraid to alter. How often do people say they are scared to move or change direction because they don't think they could cope with anything new?

We're better than we think

I remember the first few translations I was sent. The automatic reaction was always that I could never manage; it looked just too complicated and I'd be within an ace of sending it back, saying they'd have to find someone better qualified. The end result was always fine and one client told me after we'd worked together for several years that I should increase my fees.

A friend of mine in London, living with his extended family, bought a large house. They were squatting temporarily with other family members while the place was completely renovated. Builders being what they often are, nothing was progressing so it was decided that the younger brother, a shop manager, would give up his job to be on site and lend a hand where he could to get the work done. Once it was finished he needed to go back to work and his sister-in-law, who was the head of IT for a large bakery chain, told him they were looking for van drivers. He went for an interview and was immediately offered the job of transport manager. Prepared to start at the bottom, his obvious intelligence and willingness to do any kind of job paid off.

Someone else who tried a different way and won out was Hugh Chadwick, a 20-year-old student who resorted to advertising his availability for work at a busy road junction for days on end. With his large placard reading 'Please Give Me a Job' and a smiley face, he hit the jackpot by being offered a position with a renowned engineering company, and his employers can be sure that with that level of commitment they have hired someone who will be a great asset.

Free training is priceless

Something else that helps when opportunity knocks is never to turn down any sort of training—many of the things I can do have been learnt in the workplace at no cost to me. Another good bet is doing whatever task comes your way even if it isn't in your 'job description'. That way you acquire a reputation for flexibility and are top of the list when other openings arise. You think you can't do it? Well, you never know until you try and what's more important, the person who snaps up the chance may very likely not do it as well as you.

Sometimes we sell ourselves short just because we don't have sufficient confidence in our ability. When I had been living in England for a while, I went back to Geneva on a temporary contract. The first morning I answered the phone to somebody speaking in French. Panicking, I handed the receiver to my colleague who proceeded to deal with it with great aplomb. What was amusing was that she spoke hardly any French at all and I already spoke it quite fluently. That lack of confidence again. Because that's all it is; it isn't a lack of ability. When we get stuck or are scared to strike out and do it differently it's only lack of confidence; it doesn't necessarily mean we are incapable. There are plenty of courses, books and opportunities to help us work on our self-esteem and when we take the plunge we open up a whole world of new beginnings.

Every situation's a new situation

As we go through life we can often be inclined to compare a new situation with one in the past where we feel we made a mistake or took the wrong decision. The circumstances may have changed and what was right for us then is not necessarily right for us now. That's why children are so much more positive about good results: they have no past experience of unwanted outcomes on which to base their choices.

Hazel Denning, a truly inspirational lady who was still writing books into her 90s, opined that the longer we hang on to our past the less likely it is that our future will improve. She expressed the view that we can turn our lives around any time we choose.

You might say it doesn't matter—it all works out in the end— but it's those who let the memory of past failures stay in the past; those who seize the most seemingly unpromising opportunities and use them as a springboard to a successful future; they are the ones who lead charmed lives and, even more importantly, have the most fun.

SECTION 3: A Matter of Choice

A Tale of Two Systems

A program on Swiss television many years ago opened my eyes to just how lucky (or should that be 'unlucky'?) we in the West are. It consisted of a report comparing two hospitals: Geneva Cantonal Hospital and the main hospital in Burkina Faso, West Africa.

The film in Geneva was made by the Burkinabé, and the film of the hospital in their capital, Ouagadougou, was made by the Swiss. The fact that nearly 30 years have elapsed since I saw it and the fact that it has stayed in my mind shows that it really grabbed my attention.

The hospital in Ouagadougou obviously looked extremely primitive compared with our super hi-tech facilities in the West, but there is one thing that all the hi-tech and expertise in the world cannot replace. In Burkina Faso the patients' food is prepared and provided by their families who camp in the grounds of the hospital. There may not be sufficient beds, drugs, qualified staff, but they benefit from the care, love and home cooking of their families. What better recipe for getting well? In many Western hospitals long-stay patients have no or few visitors who sit wondering what to talk about and keeping an eye on the clock.

Comparisons can be astonishing

The film the Burkinabé made of the Cantonal Hospital in Geneva opened by showing a man dressing himself up in all sorts of protective clothing as if he were about to take off for the moon. A surgeon, on his way to perform open-heart surgery perhaps? No, a cleaner! The amount spent on chasing bugs in the West could build several hospitals in the Third World. We create bugs because of our lack of hygiene where it matters, and because of the overdosing of antibiotics which make germs resistant to practically any kind of treatment that presently exists. People can go into a hospital in the West for a minor operation and come out feet first because of the powerful infections that those with shot immune systems or weakened by illness or surgery can pick up. I imagine that in African hospitals you can also die of something other than the illness that put you there in the first place, but I do wonder if you're as likely to be exposed to—and this comes from a House of Commons Public Accounts Committee report issued in the UK in 2006—*blunders ranging from medication errors and drug interactions to missing emergency equipment and the wrong limbs being amputated.*

Someone I met who had recently retired told me of an experience where his mother-in-law, in hospital in one of the UK's largest cities, died suffering from malnutrition. (UK official statistics for 2011 estimate that *80 hospitalized patients a day* die from lack of basic care.) My acquaintance was so shocked that he had set up a system with other volunteers in a hospital in the small town where he lived to be present at mealtimes to help the patients who couldn't feed themselves. It was a win-win situation as the hospital just didn't have sufficient staff to ensure that the basic task of putting food into people's mouths could be covered. In the richest countries in the world, some patients only get fed if volunteers are available to help them eat their meals. And nobody asks why?

Love may be the best medicine

I have a strong feeling that if I were ill or old I would prefer to be in hospital in a country where people who love me could be counted on to be there to provide me with the food I enjoy and which I'm used to eating rather than some of the things that are dished up in Western hospitals. In 2011 a long-stay patient in a UK hospital photographed his meals and put the images on the web in the form of a quiz, asking who could guess what they were supposed to be. The dishes were extremely colorful and at first glance looked delicious but he confessed that although he was the one eating them, he couldn't identify the contents either.

There is a rider to this story in that a couple of days after writing it I was introduced to someone from Burkina Faso. I mentioned it to him and he told me that when the program was aired, viewers in Switzerland donated so much money that the hospital in Ouagadougou was not only able to purchase mattresses for the children (which had been the aim of a request for funds) but had built a whole new pediatric wing using local labor. There was even sufficient money for some of the local doctors to come to the West and train with world experts in their field, and people were still talking about it. As we have a reputation for plundering the riches of Africa, how heartening it is to learn that we have been able to put something back.

Broadening the Mind

The French translation of the expression 'Travel broadens the mind' is *Le voyage forme la jeunesse*—literally, 'Travel molds youth', but the verb can also mean 'to train' and that seems to fit the situation better as we are rarely the same after an experience way outside anything we've known before.

A visit to Africa with Caritas, the Catholic charity in the 1980s, was a totally mind-opening event for me. The only Africans I had met up to that time were those who could afford to live and work in Europe but I had no concept of Africa beyond these people and the mostly negative opinions in newspapers or disaster scenarios on television or in films.

The purpose of our trip to Senegal and Mali was to visit the Caritas projects—market gardening, well building and bush dispensaries in Senegal and, in Mali, a workshop where people learnt to repair vehicles: Caritas was also involved in well building and projects for alphabetization there. We had the privilege of meeting the local people in their homes and visiting places where tourists hadn't yet penetrated. The trip was totally unforgettable and when I returned to Senegal many years later to a small village to learn to play the *djembe* (the African drum) it was wonderful to spend time again with truly authentic and gentle people. People took no particular notice of us on our visits to the little local town and I remember a conversation with a woman carrying her baby on her back as we fell into step. The baby had been feverish but she told me he was getting better and, as our paths diverged, we went our separate ways. This was just a short exchange between two human beings, not a typical conversation between an African and a European.

And how to do it
The wealthy in centuries gone by would take the Grand Tour.

People do this today on organized trips where either they are shepherded around in flocks or looked after every minute of the day in five-star hotels from which they return home, often no wiser about the place they've visited or the people who live there than they were before.

On my way back from my *djembe*-playing holiday I had a conversation on the plane with a couple returning from a winter break in the Gambia. They told me they hadn't moved outside their hotel, complaining about the awful food they had been served. This conversation convinced me that we can go wherever we like but if our eyes are shut we might as well stay at home.

For those of us who leave our own countries to live abroad this fact does not necessarily broaden our horizons either.

I've spent half my life away from the UK, studied the local language and been able to join in activities and integrate with the local population, although this still hasn't always saved me from cultural gaffes! I've also met many people who have no desire to do so and who prefer to spend their time in the clubs and pseudo Irish and English pubs that spring up together with restaurants serving international fare; places where most people have some grasp of English and where they prefer to meet up with other expats doing the things they would probably do at home.

I can't say it's a wasted opportunity because not only is that just a personal view but many didn't necessarily choose the country where they live as they may have been sent out by their companies and are only staying for a short time anyway before moving on. Although with nations being encouraged to fight each other, where hatred for another country or race seems often to be actively encouraged, there has never been a better time to discover what we can do in our small way to find out about people in other countries, see how they live and what their traditions are.

We are all one

The Olympic Games seem to emphasize the need to win medals and gain access to the lucrative sponsorships that follow rather than just the honor of being there, although one of the upsides is that people from all over the world come together, either to compete against each other or just as spectators or workers. Lasting friendships have been struck up and even marriages have resulted from the huge melting pot.

On the other hand, mass tourism seems to be doing the opposite of opening minds and I'm not sure about eco-tourism either. I appreciate the luck I have had to mix with people from all sorts of horizons and backgrounds and look forward to the day when we stop behaving badly towards one other; when we realize that it's in our interest to work together, to celebrate our differences rather than considering them a threat to our very existence. It will happen, I'm sure of it, but we all need to do our bit to make it so.

When everything is taken into account, we are all one and if you hurt my brother or sister, you hurt not only me but yourself as well.

Divine Timing

Sometimes, however hard we try to make things happen, they just stubbornly refuse to bend to our will. There's something called divine timing which comes into play here. So what's that all about?

Well, there are often other people involved in whatever it is we want and every element has to be in place before we can all move forward. Sometimes we think life is plain sailing and along comes a hitch and things fall apart. Could it be that we are not ready for what we want to manifest? We may think we are but, only seeing a tiny fragment of the whole picture, we are extremely poor judges of what is right for us and what is not. It might even be right for us later on but not at this moment.

If we decide to consult a medium we may receive a message that within, say, a couple of months there will be a great change in our life. When the two months are up, if nothing earth-shattering has happened, we can feel very let down. This could be because time on other planes does not exist; linear time is a completely man-made thing and those giving the message are utterly unable to relate to our material world and its calendar.

While I was living abroad, a friend in England went into hospital to have an operation but was devastated to be discharged almost immediately and told to lose some weight first. This was just before my mother died suddenly and this wonderful lady was an absolute tower of strength, helping me with all the things I had to get done in the two short weeks I was able to be in the UK. Had she undergone the operation as scheduled, she wouldn't have been able to do anything. What was very sad was that she finally entered hospital two weeks after I left and died under the anesthetic. Not only was that traumatic for her family but without her good sense, her wisdom and her practical help I would have been at a total loss. Divine timing was at work again.

Meeting the right person

Sometimes whatever it is we want and work towards it's not something that is in our best interests. For example, fixing our all on attracting a particular person into our life may not be good for either of us or it may not be the right time. We hear of couples who first met when they were young, fell in love and were separated, perhaps through parental disapproval or a silly argument or one moving away. They lose touch, marry someone else and then, as if by chance, their paths cross when they are older and they discover that through divorce or death they are both now free to be together. Perhaps the years in between would have been blissfully happy or perhaps the pair would have developed in different directions and become strangers to each other. Maybe it was better to meet again when they had done their growing up.

Some years ago I was a listener with the Samaritans and heard many sad stories. At the time I had been through the mill a bit, too, so I could empathize with what I was hearing. Had I wanted to do the work at 20, with no experience of life slapping me in the face, it would have been completely the wrong time and I would have been at a loss when trying to listen empathetically to callers talking about so many things that I had not then experienced.

Holding the dream

I always have some project on hand that I really want to come to fruition. I can never see any reason why it can't work straight away, but perhaps I don't have the necessary maturity to succeed, or perhaps all the pieces of the puzzle aren't yet in place. Sometimes if we push too hard for something it doesn't work nearly as well as it would have done had we been ready to wait for the right moment. It could even be a test to see if it really is for our highest good and if it really is what we want. Whatever, we need to be utterly convinced of our desire for it and the knowledge that it is on the way and, unless something better turns up or we decide we don't want it anymore, it will arrive in its own good time and there's nothing we can do to hurry it along.

Enthusiasm

As we go through life we obviously meet all sorts of people, although the ones who make me saddest are those who seem to have no real enthusiasm for anything. They may not be poor or short of any material comforts; the fact that they are so lucky to be living with everything they need in the rich West is something in itself. In fact it often seems that the more people have in material terms the less enthusiastic they are about anything at all, with the most positive people I have ever met being those living the dream, whatever their dream may be.

Charles Kingsley put it rather well when he opined that we act as if comfort and luxury were the chief requirements in our lives when the one thing we need to make us happy is to be enthusiastic about something.

Yes, of course we need food and clean water, a roof over our heads and a means of earning a living. We need friends and people who love us, people to spend time with, people with whom we can share things, people who have the same interests, people who make us laugh. These are all basic human needs and I can remember some marvelous evenings spent with friends tossing ideas around and coming up with some really amazing solutions. When I was young and still living at home I used to sit until the wee small hours with friends in their parents' kitchens or in mine, drinking coffee, finishing all the cigarettes we could lay our hands on and passionately putting the world to rights. The ideas we came up with probably didn't survive the light of day. No matter, they got us enthusiastic about something even if just for a few hours and off we went to bed with our hopes sky high.

But where does enthusiasm come from? I wonder if it stems from our upbringing. Or does it come from our disposition? We naturally need events to make us enthusiastic, but here's the thing; there's so much about which we can enthuse.

Enthusiasm, for a lifelong passion or for an idea that comes up one day and vanishes the next, raises our spirits. It makes us forget the niggly little things that take up far too much of our energy. We can bring it to anything we do and we *should* bring it to *everything* we do.

Making things happen

A colleague told me once that his sister had dropped out of university because her goal was to live in the mountains and to be a shepherd. As she and her husband had been doing just that very happily for a number of years, she was living her dream. His brother had also dropped out of university, this time to become a musician and although he hadn't made the big time, he was totally happy with what he was doing. My colleague added that their parents felt rather proud to have children who wanted a different sort of life.

I am also reminded of some of the people who live long, long lives. What those I've come across have in common is that, although they have faced the same trials and tribulations as the rest of us, they have looked on the bright side and been enthusiastic about life and the work they do, and this could be the reason for their longevity.

Keeping the faith

A lady I first met a couple of decades ago is now 94 and as she has slowly gone blind over the past ten years, she had to give up her apartment and live in what is a very beautiful home for people with visual handicaps. I lost touch with her several years ago but someone told me recently that she was the life and soul of the place because she is so grateful for everything and always full of joy. When she does move on from here, she will have left a wonderful legacy.

Another great example is Louise Ireland-Frey who was born

in 1912, trained as a doctor and at the age of 67 went on to study hypnotherapy. Her best-known book *Freeing the Captives* was published when she was 87. In 2008, at the age of 96, she brought out a three-volume work, *Blossom of Buddha*, at which time she announced her retirement. I don't know if she is alive at the time of writing, but if she is I'm sure she's still enthusiastic about something or other and planning her next project.

Finding the Silver Lining

Congratulations. What a wonderful opportunity you've been given.

With these words Colin Caffell starts his book *In Search of the Rainbow's End*, the amazing and heart-warming story of his journey to wholeness after the brutal murder of his ex-wife and their 6-year-old twin sons. The odd phrase was said by someone to whom he had just been introduced and fortunately the courageous interlocutor crossed his path seven years after the events as he readily observes that he might have committed murder himself if it had been trotted out at the time.

Although from a safe distance I can see the truth of the remark, I know I would never, ever have had the courage to say it to him. Nor would I have been such a quick thinker either. But it is a fact that if we can see the good which comes out of evil, we are on our way to being healed.

In the early days of AIDS back in 1987 a quality Sunday newspaper sought stories from people then infected on how they were coping. One of those interviewed said he saw it as a blessing because it had caused him to take a good look at the life he had been leading and to make huge changes in order to live the way he felt he *should* have been living.

The newspaper reporter was appalled: 'Oh, no, we can't print that. That's not what our readers want.'

Several years later, when people were less shocked at such stories of triumph over misfortune, I well remember a lady who had been treated for breast cancer at an holistic cancer center because she said more or less the same thing: that it had been a blessing that had stopped her in her tracks and sent her on a totally different path.

How it works
In 1975, Martin Brofman, a Wall Street banker, was diagnosed

with terminal cancer of the spine and given two months to live. He immediately started working with meditation and affirmations; tools he would have laughed at a few months earlier. Within those eight weeks the tumor disappeared and he has spent the years since that time teaching other people how to improve their lives before they get to such a critical point.

Brandon Bays, who runs The Journey workshops and who has written a book about her own journey, took just over six weeks to get rid of an enormous tumor in her stomach by going within and trying to see how this had happened to someone who lived a totally healthy lifestyle. What she found gave her the idea to help other people and that's what she, too, has been doing ever since.

Learning where to look

What's going on? In many cases of a complete turnaround, forgiveness has been a major element and that includes forgiving ourselves as we work on forgiving everybody else. Any grudges we carry are purely in our own minds and often the person we consider as having hurt us had no intention of doing so and has no memory of the event; by refusing to forgive we are hurting ourselves more than we are hurting him or her. This is where our *un*-ease starts and it's when it gets down to a cellular level that it becomes *dis*-ease and does real harm to our bodies. When we feel hard done by; when we feel everything is against us and we can only expect trouble and heartache, that's when our lives come off the rails.

Mastering the techniques

When I did the Silva Method course for the first time our teacher suggested we say 'Fantastic' when anything seemingly negative happened to us. I was able to put this into practice one Sunday evening after doing a repeat course. I had parked my car outside the venue in central London as the meters didn't work on a Sunday. On leaving to go home it was nowhere to be seen. Did I really bring it this morning? Puzzled, I went to reception and started to tell them that my car had gone.

'Red Fiesta, was it?' interrupted the receptionist.

'Yes.' I stared at him.

'Oh, somebody crashed into it and the police towed it away.'

I opened my mouth and out came the word 'Fantastic'. He looked at me as if I'd just fallen to earth and the rest is a long story. Owning a car in London is a nuisance and when I had gone back there to live a few months earlier I had planned to sell it. I mentally thanked the driver who crashed into it because he did me a favor and I also blessed the Silva Method for giving me the tools to see it as such. Look for the silver lining, in the words of an old song, because you will always find one.

Fringe Dwellers

A group to which I belong was meeting to discuss what our options were in the months to come, on where the world is heading and, why, with all we have going for us, so many people are unhappy.

When I heard that it was to be held in the Aung San Suu Kyi room in a local center I had to smile. How appropriate! This lady has always been a heroine for me because, although you can never walk in someone else's moccasins, I feel sure I could never have made the sacrifices she has. Of course she comes from a different culture and a different background and when she married an Englishman she told him that if her country ever needed her she would have to go. Her country did and does need her and she lived through years of solitude, of being confined to her home, of knowing her husband was mortally ill and dying on another continent.

We can think of Nelson Mandela, sitting for years in a prison cell, who, on being freed on the death of apartheid in South Africa, didn't immediately look around for revenge but preached forgiveness and reconciliation and is revered as a near saint in consequence.

Look at the Dalai Lama who is so sad to see his beautiful country taken over by a violent regime doing its best to stamp out any remains of its ancient traditions and filling it up with non-Tibetans until the indigenous people are in the minority and their culture could disappear forever.

The path of peace

These thoughts came to me against a backdrop of a debate about the legality of demonstrations. Those who felt their right to free speech was being removed were outraged and those who are tired of the violent element which breaks heads and property were greatly in favor. I have my own personal view as to who or what is behind the violence that, seemingly out of the blue, can now be guaranteed to turn any peaceful demonstration into a battlefield, but that's another story.

So where's the connection? Well, Aung San Suu Kyi, Nelson Mandela and the Dalai Lama are revered all over the world for their attitude to non-violence, for the way they preach change, as did Gandhi, through everyone working together for the good of all. Can anyone remember much about the Red Brigades in Germany who wanted change through violence in the 1970s? How many people even remember their names?

If we had more?

So let me go back to my theme on why so many people are unhappy and what options we've got to improve our lives. If we had more technology? Made more money? Had a bigger car, exotic holidays, designer clothes, were one of the beautiful people? Would something like that be the answer? Well, it doesn't necessarily sound like something to aim for. To my mind the most beautiful people are not only those I've mentioned but also the hundreds and thousands, possibly millions, who are opting out of the artificial merry-go-round that is geared to take our minds off what really matters.

Stuart Wilde, an author and workshop leader, has a name for them which I rather like. He calls them (and I can say 'us' here as you will already have gathered I am much in sympathy with their ideals) 'fringe dwellers', people paying lip service to what the world's rulers would like them to believe and do but who, without fuss or fanfare, have decided to live in a way they feel is more ethical and aimed at giving a slice of the cake to everyone. It could hold the key to our future and I invite you to join us.

Liberty

Voltaire had something profound to say about many things, although the expression most often attributed to him was that he might not agree with what you say but would defend your liberty to say it. Neat though it undoubtedly is, he was apparently not the author.

So what do we mean by liberty? I think there are some cultural differences here and living in a multicultural society we come crashing up against them all the time; or at least I do. One of the main problems as I see it is noisy neighbors. This is something I have known elsewhere and unless you have a reasonably good relationship with the people around you, it can lead to tears. Or murder. There have been cases in several cities where people have been driven to the edge by constant noise and delivered their personal form of justice.

Thinking about our actions

I live on a main road and in the summer it is too hot to sleep with the windows shut. There is a pedestrian crossing below with lights that seem to work at night even when there is nobody around. This naturally stops the cars and those with windows wound down and stereo systems blasting out never fail to wake me up. And why is it that, when someone else's taste in music is being imposed on me, it is never anything I would remotely choose to listen to?

I once spent a weekend in a naturist colony in the south of France with some friends who had a small apartment there. One of them liked to walk for miles along the beach so he used to put his swimming costume under his hat and when he got to the limit of the naturist beach he would put it on to continue his stroll. Well, he would have been in trouble with the law if he hadn't, but surely it's plain courtesy, where the huge majority doesn't share your views, not to insist on doing it your way.

Our own beliefs

Liberty for our beliefs is something else to which we should all aspire. Not to foist them on other people but to be left alone to believe what we like as long it never leads to active discrimination against another individual. I remember once telling a very wise person how I felt bad about the unkind thoughts I occasionally harbored on the subject of someone whom I considered a friend. She told me that having the thoughts helped me to release whatever it was I resented so that when I was with the person concerned I had got it all off my chest and could be a proper friend. And it worked.

I think liberty is something to be earned and cherished. State-sponsored infringement of liberty has become a vast and lucrative industry and a great deal more sinister than being troubled by noisy neighbors or harboring unpleasant thoughts. We are usually told that badges, security checks and CCTV cameras everywhere are for our safety, which is highly debatable, and we are also told that being micro-chipped would be a splendid idea, but I think it is truly appalling; it would reduce us to the level of cows with their owner's mark branded on one ear.

Respecting the liberty of others

Those of us who are doing our best to make the world a better place through our words and our actions seek the liberty in which to do it. Anyone with any sense of responsibility is unlikely to encroach on the liberty of another person. Like many other people, I don't need rules and regulations to keep me in line, and one day I dream that the world will be sufficiently evolved to do away with any barrier to freedom, where we can all live in peace together, satisfied with what we have and happy to collaborate with everyone else.

Perhaps the ultimate dream of liberty is in the words of the song 'Imagine' written by John Lennon. He talks about living in peace with no wars, no possessions, no greed; a real brotherhood of man. It's a dream many people share and one day, if enough of us believe it is possible, it will come to pass.

The description of liberty that I like most was set down by John Milton, the 17th-century poet, in *Paradise Lost* and it's one we forget all too easily: *Licence they mean when they cry Liberty.* The difference between the two is like night and day.

Reincarnation

I once spent a few months working with a colleague who said something that changed my thinking radically and made me wonder if that was why I was in that job, just to hear the message she had to give.

Her husband's parents were Jewish and had met in a concentration camp, fortunately just before the end of the Second World War, and they had obviously lived to tell the tale. When she was recounting it to me she added that it was so clear to them that reincarnation was a reality because otherwise how could they make sense of the difficulties some people experience while others seem just to sail through life? It wouldn't be fair if we only had one go at it.

Looking for proof

Dr Ian Stevenson, who was working until the time he died at the age of 88, probably did more than anyone else to provide evidence of reincarnation. He traveled the world, meticulously documenting and verifying stories and checking birthmarks of children who had given clear accounts that pointed to a past life. In some of the countries where he spent time (India, Lebanon, Myanmar, Thailand) reincarnation is part of their belief systems, so it wasn't difficult to find cases. A quite different matter was amassing all the proof that he and his researchers needed before pronouncing a case to be a true reincarnation. He was first and foremost a scientist and cast-iron proof was what he was always seeking; until he had it, no case was considered to have been solved.

Carol Bowman, who is one of the world's top researchers into children's past-life memories, has written a couple of excellent books; one is entitled *Children's Past Lives* where she tells us how she discovered why her son was terrified of loud noises and why her daughter was terrified of fire. The book in itself is quite amazing and offers some thought-provoking stories of children with very clear memories of an earlier life or lives. She followed this up with something even more jaw-dropping entitled *Return from Heaven: Beloved Relatives Incarnated within Your Family.* As the title suggests, here she deals with cases of children who have reincarnated into families in which they lived previously. Sometimes replacing a dead child, sometimes coming back as their own grandson or granddaughter; whatever the case, the child was either recognized immediately or when it started to talk would come out with the kind of statements that left its family in no doubt at all as to its identity.

What religion teaches

From a religious point of view, opinions differ although most of the folk religions as well as Buddhism and Hinduism are firm believers in reincarnation. The Islamic mystics the Sufis, and the Jewish mystics the Kabbalists, all believe in reincarnation, too, and it was included in the Catholic Apocrypha and taught in the Catholic Church until the Council of Constantinople in 553 AD when it was voted out on the orders of Emperor Justinian. Naturally a belief that we had many opportunities in which to right all our mistakes would take too much power from the established church which had a vested interest in getting us to do as it dictated. That meant that any deviation from the path the church wished people to follow would result in eternal damnation.

Through the huge number of books being published on the subject and the information available on the Internet, many people have come to examine it a little more closely and debates about reincarnation rage in all sorts of unexpected places. This can only be healthy.

Whatever our beliefs, all will become clear when we leave this planet and go on to the next step. Some of us will be confused; some disbelieving; and some will receive the confirmation of what they were expecting, whatever that might be.

Renewal

Every March, the start of a new year is an exciting time to be alive with two important events taking place as nature starts to wake up and stretch its limbs.

But don't we have New Year's Day in January? Well, according to the fairly recent Gregorian calendar, we do. However, the Chinese, Tibetans, Hindus, Iranians, Thais, Jews, Muslims have completely different dates, invariably coinciding with the phases of the moon, and many shamanic cultures celebrate the New Year on 21 March, the first day of spring for us in the northern hemisphere; this is far more logical when you think about it than the first day of January which is in the middle of a season and has no special meaning.

When midnight on 31 December booms out and everyone goes crazy, it only happens to a slice of the world's population at a time. This was brought home to me on New Year's Eve 1999 when I waited excitedly for the countdown to the brand-new millennium in Switzerland with a bunch of other people and realized that in London there was still an hour to go and in Australia people were probably recovering from the New Year's Day celebrations. It took away all the awe of the occasion to realize that we weren't celebrating together, just small groups of people taking it in turns.

Nature awakes

The first day of spring is a different matter. We have 24 hours to ease ourselves gently into the new season rather than waiting for some iconic clock to strike the hour. We can *see* nature waking up everywhere and even those who scoff at the thought of a new year starting on 21 March can't deny that something is happening with the shoots coming into flower. We can almost hear it. Our clocks change too, giving us some extra daylight.

The ancient Greeks held their festival of the sun in the spring to celebrate the hatching of the world. In days gone by the winters were extremely harsh, so it was only then that the sun started to shine more warmly, the trees and flowers came into bud and the hibernating animals woke up after their long winter sleep.

Another extremely important event taking place around the same time is the festival of Eostre, the Pagan goddess of Easter. Her name is related to the word 'east', making her a dawn goddess and her feast is linked to the cycles of the moon: according to ancient beliefs, the moon has always been a symbol of the divine feminine energy. The Easter bunny symbolizes the fertility of the awakened world and the Easter egg symbolizes rebirth. In Berne, the Swiss capital, there used to be a bear pit in the town center and Easter was traditionally the time when big crowds gathered to catch a glimpse of the newborn cubs.

Shedding our winter skins

This is an important time for us, too, as we shed our winter clothes and start to make plans and perhaps new resolutions, such as detoxing (which, whatever the beauty gurus say, should only be done in spring when kidney energy is at its highest), getting in shape for the summer, eating more salads and fewer chips, taking up an outdoor sport. It means finding time to get outside and work in the garden or, if you don't have one, at least go for a walk in the nearest park and see the natural world waking up, listen to the fledglings cheeping and give thanks that the frosts and snows of another winter have done their job of protecting the work that's gone on while the earth has seemingly been asleep.

With all this happening at the same time, how can anyone imagine that the real new year starts on the first day of January?

Sense and Sensitivity

Working at home one day a year or so ago, the doorbell rang around midday and a Senegalese neighbor from the floor below stood there holding a steaming dish of lamb.

It was the festival of *Eid al Adha* and, as a good Muslim, she had prepared food for her neighbors. I didn't know about the custom but apparently her religion requires her to offer a dish of lamb, ritually killed for the occasion, to the people who live around her. The problem is that I don't eat meat. So I imagined that I had explained the situation sensitively and honestly. Many months later a secular Arab told me that I had been totally wrong and should never have refused it even if it ended up in the garbage bin and I'd been forced to lie by telling her it was delicious.

I felt so bad about what I'd done as we have a lot of respect for each other that, when a couple of days later I ran into her, I immediately brought the subject up. To my horror she told me that she and her daughters had been really hurt and tears came into her eyes as she remembered it. She had tried to explain to them that as I was European I probably didn't understand their customs. According to her I should have taken it and given it to someone else. But who? She mentioned an African student I had had a while before but I could hardly keep it in case he came back for a lesson! When I told her I could only have put it in the garbage bin she was horrified and said that that would have been terrible. Politeness would have dictated that I praise the dish, thereby opening the way for a repeat the following year.

And then, thinking on it a few hours later, I stopped feeling guilty. Switzerland, where I have lived for many years, is a secular country that forbids ritual killing and, although *Eid al Adha* is an official United Nations holiday, I'm sure that most people have no idea that offering food to neighbors is *de rigueur*.

We know about people fasting in Ramadan but that's about it. If this had happened in Africa, of course things would have been different but although I had unwittingly hurt her feelings, it was really due to the way she had perceived it as a slight.

Our views matter too

My personal view is that animals shouldn't really be killed for us to eat and the idea of cutting the throat of a sheep or lamb and leaving it to bleed to death is quite awful.

When my English class has its end-of-year picnic I always have to impress upon the students from Asia that they mustn't bring a dish with pork as there are invariably one or two Muslims and I like the whole class to be able to share each other's food.

Living in a multicultural society is rich indeed, but in any society life can be a minefield and although we try to understand and cater for other people's customs and beliefs, we can't be blamed if they conflict with our own. That would be tantamount to saying that one view of life is more important than another and although my neighbor was hurt, my feelings counted too and another idea came to me about this. Are those of us in cities so used to living side by side with people from every country you care to name that we don't notice the differences anymore and are quite startled when someone seems to adhere to another culture? I'd like to think it's that and perhaps one day it will be the case everywhere.

Taking Our Power Back

So what is power? We hear the word all the time as something to be coveted by just about anyone, especially politicians. We talk about someone being in power in one country or another and we hear about politicians seeking power by standing for election. It seems to be something that people only give up when it's forcibly wrested from their grasp. We hear about power at gunpoint as if we have to threaten and kill to get our hands on this desirable commodity.

It is so sought after because it seems to bring with it all the goodies of life. The people who elect the politicians may be left to their own devices but those in power lead a charmed life, and this is probably true of just about every country on the planet. Being in power means not having to justify one's decisions and actions to anyone else and because it *is* so heady, it's something to hold on to for as long as possible for those who have it and something to acquire by any means for those who don't.

But that's not real power, because those in power are never there forever, even in a dynastic dictatorship, and they usually have to watch their backs all the time to ensure things stay as they are. Enough to give them sleepless nights!

So what is *real* power?

The only power that *really* matters is something that we all possess and how many of us seem happy to give it away all the time? When we stick to a job we don't like because the salary's good, that's giving our power away to our employer; when we stay with a relationship that is past its sell-by date, that's saying that we might never attract anyone else and we'll end up on our own; when we have to ask everyone else for their opinion before we make a decision, that's saying that our own isn't worth much and everybody else knows better. Of course we can then blame them if it all goes wrong!

Ah, the blame game. How often do we read about people looking for someone to blame? The boss, the government, the council, the media, the family, the neighbors; they're all responsible for making us unhappy, making us do silly things or taking something from us. It's very easy because we don't have to change; we just wish *they* would.

It is very scary to go out on a limb, but just think: when our lives become something we construct ourselves, we can't rely on anyone else to put things right. When we can live with our mistakes because we know we can pick ourselves up and go off in a different direction, we aren't beholden to anyone. We are all immeasurably powerful but, through listening to other people or reading the doom and gloom peddled by the media, we don't believe it. The politicians, the press barons and those in power have a vested interest in making us feel fearful, weak and worthless, but people everywhere are beginning to wake up and take their power back and that is the nightmare of all those whom we have allowed to wield their spurious form of power over us.

The Southern Way of Death

Scrolling down a classical music website looking for some music to listen to while I worked, I came across something called *Between the Ears*, a magazine program, with that week's offering being a snapshot of a small radio station and the local community it serves in Mount Airey, North Carolina. Like many local radio stations in that part of the world the staple fare is news, gospel music and firebrand preachers, but the specialty of WPAQ 740AM is that three times a day local obituary notices are read out, each with a potted biography of the person who has died. One very important factor seems to be that the broadcasters reading the obituaries know how to give the names the proper local pronunciation and before they go on air the text is carefully proofread to get things just right. Sounds pedantic, but it means a lot to the families, as if the reader had a more personal contact with their loved ones.

At first the idea of broadcasting obituaries may seem extremely morbid, but after listening to the program it strikes me as a very healthy way of dealing with death. I don't think there's a culture on the planet that does not need closure, which is why we have so many different types of ceremony depending on where we live and what we believe.

Obtaining closure

When there has been a war, a plane or boat accident, an unsolved murder, a natural disaster (the tsunami in Asia for example) or, indeed, any circumstance where the relatives have no body to bury or cremate, they can suffer long-term grief. According to some belief systems, unless the prescribed ceremonies have been completed, the survivors worry that their loved ones won't have found the way to where they need to go and are condemned to wander the astral plane forever. When museums in the West have been shamed into giving back to shamanic cultures the human artifacts they stole over a century ago, a major ceremony is always held to help that person's soul pass finally through the veil that separates their world from ours.

The obituary notice slot on WPAQ 740AM started several years ago when the local paper was not published so frequently. In such a small community everyone knows everyone else but by the time the paper came out the funeral had often already taken place. Those interviewed all mentioned the word 'closure' as they listened to the obituaries, and, whether the deceased had been a prominent member of the community or a humble toiler, they liked the fact that no difference was made by the broadcaster, and the one who was interviewed on the program felt he was doing an important job. Even those who had lost close family members found that hearing their obituaries read out made it somehow more real, made it finally sink in.

In other cultures people would probably laugh out loud at such an idea because for them death is part of life and there's nothing particularly tragic or unusual about it. However, for us in the West where we prefer to sweep it under the carpet and talk about it as little as possible, closure is just as important and a respectful announcement on a radio station that everyone in the community listens to is proving to be a very effective way of helping people come to terms with it.

When Life Changes

Are you good at endings? I have so much trouble with them. Whether it's a job, a relationship, a friendship, it has always been hard. Surprisingly, moving home has never been a challenge. I don't mean the dreary and stressful job of packing and unpacking; that's invariably awful. There have been places (usually countries) I haven't wanted to leave; purely from a nostalgic point of view although they held nothing more for me at that particular time, but moving around in the same city is invariably accompanied by euphoria at having somewhere better to live.

No, it's the other things. Recently I was in a situation where I was doing rather a lot of work for a large organization. It was a place I had worked many times before and it was lovely being back in the swing with former colleagues. The salary was excellent and the work not at all demanding and even quite interesting. So why did I wake up every morning with a slight sinking feeling? It just wasn't what I knew I was supposed to be doing, that's why. As the work dried up, the end came anyway, but all the good times and the laughs (and the thought of the regular income!) came back to me and I had to tell myself very sternly to shut the door and leave space for another one to open.

Moving on

We often want life to change, to move on, but, without letting go of the trapeze, we drag our feet and stick with the known and the humdrum. I've seen it so many times with people in jobs that are more or less for life. They would like to do something else but the money and security are like a ball and chain and it is very tough indeed, even when you have few financial or family commitments, to let go. I've been there, too, cheering myself up by telling myself that the money I earn enables me to attend workshops and events I couldn't have afforded otherwise. There is also the worry that if you have spent 20 years in one type of job, adapting to something totally new could be too demanding.

Another difficult area is relationships. When couples break up it is frequently one partner deciding to leave the other, but even if the decision is mutual, it causes a great deal of pain to everyone concerned. I have been on both sides and, once when I was very young, felt such a terrible sense of guilt at making someone unhappy that I stayed too long in a relationship that was dead. I also remember other occasions, one when I was the person left and was devastated. A couple of weeks before one break I was watching out of the window for my other half to arrive one evening with a sinking feeling that was quite new. I was probably picking up on his reluctance at being with me and we really had come to the end of our path together, but it was a very painful experience.

The end of a friendship

Platonic friendships are another thing. Sometimes we move on and our friends don't want to follow us, but they don't want the friendship to end either and we don't know how to do it gently. Changing direction so many times, I'm extremely bad about ending a friendship that really has run its course and have been known to take the cowards' way out; when a friend and I have absolutely nothing left to talk about and we tiptoe round each other to avoid contentious subjects, it has needed more courage than I possess to be honest and I have finally become unavailable. Sometimes I realize that a friend has started to become elusive, and that's when I need to release any expectations and let that person continue on life's path without me.

My feeling is that we are all on a journey and situations, jobs and people cross our paths and are perfect for who we are at each moment, just as we are perfect for that passage in their lives; we aren't meant to contort ourselves into an alien shape just to hang on and neither are they. People who have given us a hard time have been teaching us something priceless and if we don't learn the lesson then it will come back through someone else until we do. So I'm trying to make my endings as gentle as possible, being honest with myself about a job that no longer holds a future, or a friendship that has come to an end, and release them with love and gratitude for what they have brought me and what they have taught me.

Why Do We Say These Things?

'The flight before yours has been canceled because of high winds. You're going to have a horrible journey.'

For a nervous flyer, being greeted by the assistant at the check-in desk at London's Heathrow Airport with these words was the last thing I needed. And it made me wonder. Why do we say things like that when we know they're more than likely going to upset the listener?

I have heard people mention to someone that the doctor has diagnosed a health problem or that they are going into hospital for an operation and the other person has replied either with a tale of how awful it was for them or how they know someone who had the same thing and it was a terribly painful experience.

Sometimes we have a genuine desire to impart information and are just tactless, opening our mouths before we know whether the other person wants to hear our pearls of wisdom or not; sometimes taking a malign pleasure in saying something we know will cause pain. And I have been as guilty as the next one. I invariably feel very bad about it afterwards and sometimes the shame of the pain caused comes back to me years later and I cringe at how nasty I can be.

Knowing what's appropriate

One of my faults, although a friend seems to think it's amusing, is an unfortunate tendency to say the wrong thing. Expressing unasked-for opinions, without qualifying them with 'Well, it's just my opinion' (or better still, keeping my mouth shut), they come out like statements: saying how I find spotted dogs ugly when the person to whom I'm chatting has a Dalmatian which I hadn't remembered, or green bathrooms are depressing when once again I've forgotten that the person to whom I'm giving the benefit of my opinion has a green bathroom. Either from the look on the person's face or a sudden flash of memory about that particular bathroom, I then try to dig myself out of the hole by saying something like: 'Oh, I don't mean the pretty light green you've chosen, oh no, that's lovely. What I mean is that horrible spinach green that makes a room so dark.'

The biggest howler I ever uttered was in a meeting attended by a couple of hundred people when I made a derogatory remark to my neighbor about a very short man who was taking a seat on the platform. As she was of normal height, how was I to know that, out of all those there, he was her husband?

On holiday in Scotland, watching a thousand pipers wending their way through the streets of Dunoon as a prelude to the Highland Games, how could I know that the kilted Scot whose bandy legs made me laugh out loud was the brother of the man standing next to me? Apart from the thousand pipers there must have been a few thousand onlookers and I had to pick that particular place to stand. The man fortunately thought it funny, too, as apparently the family was always teasing his brother about the sight of his legs in a kilt. Both comments were spontaneous but totally unnecessary and left me with egg on my face.

Sometimes silence is golden

Yes, our lack of tact or a need to express an opinion about everything under the sun (whether welcome or not) can hurt people without our meaning to, but what's much worse is when we say something that we know will hurt. When this happens we are often feeling pain for which we blame the other person, perhaps envy, or, and this is really a nasty one and it's embarrassing even to be admitting it, a spurious feeling of superiority ('I don't have that problem so I'm better than you'). What we are really saying is that we're not OK, although we're trying to put up a façade at that moment and we're taking it out on the first person who crosses our path. It is said that hurt people hurt people and that about sums it up.

Whatever the reason, our comments either come back to haunt us or we will very probably be on the receiving end ourselves sometime and we won't like it one bit. Is it better to be right than to be loved? Because we're all imperfect people we're going to slip now and then, that's human nature. I'm trying to learn not only to curb my tongue but to endeavor to be less critical. After all, I'm not necessarily right; my opinion is just that, my opinion—one among many, it is by no means always welcome and is often much better kept to myself.

SECTION 4: Roots

Back to Our Roots

There's a lot to be said for going back to our roots. In times of recession and crisis, whether we buy into the general mood of the moment or not, people tend to talk about going back to their roots; those who aren't trying to hang onto something that is about to disappear anyway. And it takes a huge dose of courage to let go.

So what are our roots? Are they our families? Where we were born? Where we grew up? Where we've spent a major part of our lives? In times gone by people stayed in the town or village of their birth and certainly didn't ask themselves existential questions. Life was easy or hard depending on your station in life and you got on with the hand dealt to you.

Where the heart is

There have been cases of people from developing countries who have made their homes, married and had children in the West, but whose official documents aren't in order. Despite a brave fight by their many friends and supporters, they are often expelled and sent to live somewhere they no longer know and which the children may not even have visited. The roots they have put down are torn up and it must take a huge amount of adjustment and heartache to try and plant them somewhere else.

So our roots are our 'papers', that needless bureaucracy which swaddles us from birth to the grave and provides millions of jobs? What it says on a document? Is that who we are? An astrologer friend once told me that his sister's rising sign was a planet that shows up for only a short period in our hemisphere and for much longer over Australia, where she had gone to live with no thoughts about coming back. Her official documents say she's British, but she considers that her real roots are on the other side of the world.

I've spent half my life in Switzerland and, yes, I have put down roots in a way. Oh, I love going back to London and, funnily enough, one of the things I most like about my visits is hearing people speak just like me. If I lived in London, though, I would probably feel like an alien—I know I've tried it, going back to the part of London where I took my first steps, and a good few months had to pass, mostly in the company of people from other countries, before I got the hang of things and began to feel at home.

Do we all need roots?

Sometimes the lack of real roots bothers me and here's a strange thing. A while back, trawling the Internet one wet Sunday afternoon with nothing much else to do, I decided to check out the pub where I spent many happy (and drunken) lunchtimes and evenings when I lived with my parents. There I came across a link to The World Famous Brocket Babies. What's this? Hey, I was born there! Brocket Hall, situated in the same village as the pub, was put into service as a maternity home from 1939 for a dozen years.

The antics of the present Lord Brocket brought it into the news a few years ago. As all records of the babies born there were destroyed in a fire, Brocket Baby and her husband decided to set up a website to try and find as many other Babies as possible.

Now that appears to be an extremely tenuous root, something that I can't possibly remember, but it pleases me enormously and as I drink my morning coffee out of a mug in a limited edition with *Brocket Baby* printed across an image of the Hall and grounds, it gives me a real kick that has nothing to do with the caffeine.

Being in the Flow

The room was small with 20 or 30 people managing to find a place to sit. The lady leading the evening workshop told each of us to think of the most important attribute for a happy and successful life and, after giving us a few minutes, went round the group to ask us individually what we had come up with.

Some of us had similar desires such as total trust, more patience, being kinder, etc. Some had different wishes, such as more time, a loving partner, a good job. She listened to everybody and then told us that what we all wanted amounted to the same thing. What could that be?

'You're all saying that what you really want is to be in the flow,' she told us. 'That's when all these things can come into your lives naturally without strain or stress.'

This was a few years ago and the message has stayed with me. Yes, she was right and I have proved it to myself again and again. When I am more trusting, patient, a nicer, more smiley person, things automatically seem to go well. Oh, it's easy when we're in a good space, I know.

Maintaining the flow

As a self-employed Jill of many types of work, why is it that when I land something interesting and well-paid, another job invariably falls straight into my lap?

Sometimes so many people need work done—and it's always urgent—that I start to panic about the lack of time to do it all. Why, when I finish a contract, can I sometimes wonder when the next job will appear? Feast or famine = not being in the flow.

There's something else happening here too. Although I can feel totally positive about life and know that work will come in its own time; although I know I shall never be in want and am always looked after, there seems to be something stuck deep down in some corner that is still logged on to the old pattern and it is only when I get a job that the switch clicks over and says that I'm open for business. If I were able to stay in the flow all the time my life would be so much simpler and I'd have fewer grey hairs, although I have been working on it for a good few years now and have taken fairly large strides in the right direction. Like most paths it's only when we look back on how far we have come that we notice the difference from how we used to be.

Somebody once likened the times we're out of the flow to putting our hands in the ocean and making fists to try and keep hold of the water. Of course, we're left with nothing when we open them. The only thing to do is let our hands stay open and receptive and feel the water flowing through them. Giving and receiving, not minding what happens, knowing that we're guided and protected on the higher planes. Easier said than done sometimes, but it is vitally important to our personal development that we take it on board.

Things come and go in life and we need to understand that and to know we are never alone. There is a quote from Krishnamurti which seems to sum it up: *This is my secret. I don't mind what happens.* Don't get me wrong. I'm not saying here that we should take a fatalistic attitude and sit back letting whatever happens happen; we need to do the groundwork first.

The practical stuff matters too

Concert pianists don't just sit and hope; they practice, practice and then practice again. What Krishnamurti really means is that when we have done all the groundwork—and that includes spiritual, mental and physical groundwork—and covered for every eventuality, we can relax and leave the rest up to the universal mind or whatever belief system we subscribe to which tells us there is a greater power out there. Tough stuff to put into practice, but when we can get to that place we are in the flow, open and receptive to everything life has to offer. Trust, patience, kindness, more time, a loving partner, a good job? Yes, being in the flow means achieving all this and so much more.

Bringing People Together

Ashley Banjo is an extremely motivating and motivated young man. He is the son of a Nigerian former boxer and an English former ballet dancer who run a dance studio. Although he has studied and obtained completely different qualifications, he also does some teaching at his parents' studio, he dances and he has set up a group of street dancers called Diversity who made a hit with the public in the UK after winning a TV talent competition a few years ago.

Although obviously benefiting from training at an early age, that's not the only reason why Banjo is such an amazing person. Handsome, articulate and charismatic, he's a superb choreographer and the group he has brought together consists of his brother and the lads he has known all his life, including two other sets of brothers. They are of different ages, from different racial and economic backgrounds, and when the group started some were still at school, at university. What Banjo has done is create a family that crosses every barrier set up for young people. His group is highly motivated, they have a goal in life and they are friends. He is the perfect ambassador for youth and Diversity deserves to go from strength to strength.

It's happening all over the world

There are millions of other groups of people doing all kinds of things together all over the world, not just dancing but with other interests in common, who are crossing these man-made barriers that endeavor to keep us apart. There are all kinds of nationalities coming together as life partners or work colleagues and finding that the differences are often very superficial. We don't hear much about them unless they have a particular talent or find themselves in a particular situation that hits the headlines, but they are out there.

For example, during the height of 'the troubles' in Northern Ireland, groups of Catholic and Protestant children were offered holidays together in England and discovered to their absolute amazement that, under the tribal labels and the conditioning they had received, they were the same with the same hopes and fears and aspirations for the future. We hear little about these exchanges and I'm sure they have had an effect on hundreds of young people in that troubled province.

Music plays a part too

The much-fêted East-West Divan orchestra set up by Daniel Barenboim, an Argentinian Jew and the late Edward Said, a Palestinian Christian, brings together young people from both sides of the political divide, not only from Israel and Palestine but from Egypt, Lebanon, Syria and Jordan. According to its founders, its aim is to educate, not to convert, and they play to packed houses all over the world. Barenboim holds honorary Palestinian citizenship as a tribute to his work.

Another example of bringing people together and transforming their lives through music is El Sistema, set up in 1975 in Venezuela by a former politician, José Antonio Abreu, whose name is not a household word in the West but should be. A publicly funded, voluntary musical education program enabling children from the poorest backgrounds to learn to play an instrument, it has been supported by successive Venezuelan governments. Its youth orchestras are famous the world over and musicians who learned their art through the training offered by El Sistema now play in and direct some of the top orchestras. Of the nearly 400,000 children who attend its program at any one time, it is estimated that around 70 to 90 per cent come from disadvantaged backgrounds and their involvement in music has kept them away from the drugs and alcohol which are rife in the shanty towns all over Latin America. The children start young and learn on cardboard instruments before they are entrusted with real ones. Their enthusiasm and devotion to learning are a joy to watch, a film has been made of them and the program has now been extended to the USA and the UK.

Let's look at the links

So what is the common link here? There are a couple. One is the bringing together of young people raised to distrust, fear and possibly despise those who don't have the same ideas, skin color or economic background or who don't come from the same racial group. Once they meet and work at a shared activity, they can more easily focus on the things they *do* have in common and not the differences that have always kept them apart.

The other is that whether children are academically talented or not, music in all its forms seems to have the effect of forming them into a team and the fact of dancing in a group or playing in an orchestra proves to be a bonding experience where each of them has to rely on everyone else.

In the end we are all one

People are just people the world over and there is nothing remotely new about this; at all ages they have found their differences melt away when joining in an activity with those they have been taught to consider their enemies, finding to their amazement that the enemy is just like them and when engaged in an activity together they can easily become friends. It is something that we should do our best to encourage by setting an example, as our greatest hope for a peaceful, harmonious and loving future is in the hands of our young people.

Energy

This is a word that means different things to different people. A few years ago it meant X's breakfast cereal giving you energy to start your day or Y's chocolate bar giving you a mid-afternoon boost.

Well, it still does, although we now know that this isn't really energy at all; the boost is artificial and short-lived and too much sugar has a negative effect on our bodies and especially our teeth.

Then there came the trend for health clubs which are still popular and, because sports and rapid movement stir up our adrenaline and stimulate our endorphins (the feel-good hormone), they give us the energy to do something we may not have wanted to do and they make us feel happier. Even scrubbing the kitchen floor can give us an energy boost! Once stimulated the endorphins help us to see life in a brighter light although nothing has changed physically; it's just that our energy levels have risen and we feel better all round.

Looking at it in another way

Then in New Age circles people started talking about energy in a different way. Even now, depending on the audience, it can provoke eye rolling or outright sniggering. But the truth is we all feel energy, mostly without realizing it, knowing what it is or being able to define it. 'You could have cut the atmosphere with a knife'; we've all heard that expression and experienced it ourselves. For example, two people in an embrace who have jumped apart or two people having an argument when there's a knock and the door opens. An unmistakable sense of something hidden—the energy (the feeling) in the room is tangible.

We know we like being with certain people and not with others and it isn't necessarily based on common interests but more to do with compatible energies. Some places make us feel good and some we can't wait to leave. In our homes, everything that has happened has become impregnated in the fabric of the walls and a sensitive person can read this and clear the energy that has been left behind by a former resident. Any time you live somewhere where people have suffered from illness, unhappiness, violence, the place can feel cold and unwelcoming. Where people have been happy and there has been lots of love and laughter the atmosphere seems light. When you go into a great cathedral there is something in the air; a hushed reverence, the energy of all the prayers and the singing that have become impregnated into the fabric, emanating a wonderfully calming vibration.

A study was once done in a city in the USA after the crime rate had been measured and for two weeks a group of people meditated just on raising the energy levels. At the end of the experiment it was measured again and the crime rate had dropped considerably. Once the study ended, it went back to its usual level.

In the 1980s the BBC produced a documentary on the Kogi Indians of Colombia and the Kogis chose Alan Ereira, producer and historian, to spread their message to the world. He wrote a book and went round giving talks about them. I heard him speak in London and one thing he said really struck me. One of the Mamas (elders) told him that they used to be in (energetic) communication with people all over the world but now these links were broken. 'Have you heard of a place called Tibet?' he asked Ereira. 'We used to be in contact with people there but we can't seem to hear them anymore.'

What quantum physics has to say

There is another way of looking at energy. Healers work with it. They link into the universal source and channel healing energy down to their patients through their hands—with remarkable results most of the time. So what is this energy? To say there's a lot of it about is the understatement of the century; it is everything. It's my computer, the table on which it stands, the fingers I use to type, the idea for this piece, the eyes you're using to read it. The universe is made up of energy; and the reason it takes different forms is due to its vibration. When it's vibrating very slowly it appears solid like a table and at the other end of the scale it's invisible to the naked eye and can only be felt when we tune into it, connect with it, feel it in the palms of our hands when we rub them together briskly and then slowly draw them apart.

Because everyone and everything in the universe is plugged into this energy, because we are all made of it, it must follow that each one of us is connected to everyone else. In fact healers working on a patient who is not in the same room or even the same country often report better results than from physical contact healing. Quantum physics has done the most to prove this theory of simultaneous energy transmission from one place to another completely unconnected place (from the healer to a patient in another town or country) and it is known as a quantum leap. In popular parlance, a quantum leap has come to mean a huge step forward but its real meaning is something else; it is when one electron (energy) in one place suddenly turns up somewhere completely unexpected and where logically it shouldn't be able to go.

Kirlian photography was discovered by two Russians many years ago where the hand is placed on a magnetic plate and the aura (the electromagnetic field) around it, seen as sparks of light or dull patches, is interpreted. It has been shown that people who have a limb amputated suffer what are known as 'phantom pains' in something that is no longer there. Physically it has gone but the energy field stays for a while before it, too, fades away and that is where the pain is lodged: phantom limb but real pain. Experiments have been done with leaves, where a part of a leaf has been torn away and it can be seen that the energy field stays round the whole leaf, only gradually fading from the part that has gone.

Raising the vibration

It is a sobering thought that we are connected to everyone else in the universe, that when we feel good we are helping to raise the vibrations of everyone else. When we feel bad or do something less than kind we are lowering these vibrations. Not only does it leave us with a sense of responsibility for trying to do our best at all times but it makes us realize how powerful and important each and every one of us is in the great scheme of things and how sufficient people thinking positively can change the world.

Hands across the World

Listening to a recent program, I was absolutely carried away by a wonderful story of how one Welshman made a big difference to many lives in Birmingham, Alabama.

During the worst of the civil rights riots in the 1960s, a Baptist church attended by a uniquely black congregation was blown up and four little girls on the threshold of adolescence were killed. Not only that but the church was demolished and the stained glass windows smashed.

John Potts, an artist in Wales who worked with stained glass, heard about this and was very touched by the tragedy. He racked his brains as to what he could do for the people in this congregation and he ran several ideas past his wife who became so exasperated she told him to stop talking and start doing something concrete.

He finally came up with the idea of a stained glass window which he wanted to be a gift to the church from the people of Wales. He requested donations from the public and only extremely modest sums were accepted as he insisted that it should be a people's project and not one paid for by one rich person.

The window depicts a figure in the form of a black Christ on the cross but with his arms raised and the palms upward. The idea that Christ could be black was quite horrifying to some, but the window has now become absolutely iconic and is one of the sights of Birmingham.

We may not have an artistic bone in our bodies but this little story does show that we can all make a difference and there are plenty of different ways in which we can do that.

How we can lend a hand

If you check the Internet you will find dozens of non-governmental organizations (NGOs) and some of the smallest of these, although not by any means all, are doing sterling work on an absolute shoestring. They rely on unpaid interns and volunteers to assist with administrative tasks, and private donors for much of their funding, and they are making a difference even if it is only a drop in the ocean.

For example, one which I know well works with unaccompanied minors from the developing world, not only helping them to return to their families but assisting them for the first couple of years in getting started professionally, rather than just sending them back and abandoning them. Of course they can only help a tiny minority of those in need, but they are doing something.

Another NGO I know seeks sponsors to pay for children in Rwanda to attend school. The sum for ensuring an education for a child is minimal to us in the West but it represents a fortune for them. These children are only able to attend school if they have proper clothes, and some of the pupils who have finished their schooling have been trained as dressmakers and tailors so that they can provide suitable garments instead of the rags many of them wear. The young people are given sewing machines and thereby have a means of earning their living that would not have been open to them otherwise. The NGO has also financed projects for latrines, desks for the classrooms and the provision of a goat each for some of the orphans who are now heading families so that they can derive an income. The lady who runs the NGO drives a very hard bargain with the authorities and there is no question of greasing any palms. There are thousands and thousands of vulnerable children in Rwanda and she can only help a tiny minority. But, again, it's something.

Several years ago I had the opportunity of visiting a village school in North Africa while I was on a trekking holiday. It was way out in the desert and the children were polite and really keen to learn. Their teacher was so proud of them and when we left I truly had tears in my eyes at the poverty of their equipment. I wasn't the only one to be moved by the experience, and before leaving the country, we collected money among ourselves to buy books, pens and pencils for the children. Most of what happens goes unreported as the media are much more focused on what's wrong with the world and impending catastrophes and it is only by traveling or investigating that we find out about the better side of human nature.

Striking a balance

It is difficult to strike a balance because we in the West shouldn't give the idea that we are all wealthy and that people in developing countries only have to hold out their hands. That's demeaning and certainly helps nobody. So what's the solution? The first element is respect. Respect for ourselves and respect for our fellow humans who have as much right to a secure and happy future as we do. Another is working hand-in-hand with the local populations to build the future together; the survival of the planet depends on our pulling in the same direction and not doing our utmost to see what we can get out of it.

Otherwise I really don't know and I'm not sure that anyone does. But of one thing I am convinced and it is that when we start caring about people who have so much less than we do or people to whom we can give a helping hand to pull themselves up, not only do their lives become more meaningful but so do ours.

Happy Dachnik Day

Something amazing is happening in Russia and the surrounding countries, even Chechnya, and it is now growing and spreading all over the world, although the mainstream press has not a word to say about it. Families are going back to working the land and harvesting mind-boggling quantities of fruit and vegetables using only eco-friendly methods. The annual celebration, Dachnik Day (or Gardeners' Day) is on 23 July each year when the dachniks get together and celebrate the abundance of nature.

So what's a *dachnik*? Russians for generations have clung to the idea of their family *dacha*—a little house in the country where they can escape from the pressures of town life. In Soviet times dachas were for the wealthy and well-placed, but things have now radically changed, thanks in part to Vladimir Putin, strange as that may seem.

Official encouragement

In 2003 the then President Putin signed into law the Private Garden Plot Act giving all Russians the right in perpetuity to a free plot of land on which to build a small dwelling and to plant fruit and vegetables. Plot sizes vary but are normally between 1 and 3 hectares. These plots were granted initially on the most unproductive soil but the dachniks have taken to them enthusiastically and they have developed into eco-villages.

Putin wasn't being altruistic here because at that time Russia was facing famine and, by giving people the right and the incentive to grow their own food, disaster and possibly food riots could be averted. He was obviously aware that already in 1999, 35 million small family plots, worked with enormous dynamism but without any kind of artificial fertilizer or GMO, produced 90 per cent of Russia's potatoes, 77 per cent of its vegetables, 87 per cent of its fruit, 59 per cent of its meat, 49 per cent of its milk, which is no small achievement and shows how people are inspired to work when there is an incentive to produce. With official sanction and the right to acquire land, the movement has grown and spread rapidly.

Thousands of people have left their lives in the city and moved full time to their dachas; others spend every weekend and all their holidays working their plots. I have even read about a wealthy entrepreneur who had no time to acquire and work a plot himself but who wanted fresh fruit and vegetables. He met an elderly lady, Nadezhda Ivanovna, selling her produce by the side of the road and, after tasting her home-made pickles, he bought everything she had to sell and gave her a lift home. Seeing that she lived in poor conditions, he made her an offer. He would build a house for her in a clean environment with 2000 square meters of land. He would present her with the deeds of the house and a contract obliging him to pay her 300 US dollars per month. Her job? She had to provide him and his family with all the fruit and vegetables from the land, apart from those she needed for herself. The entrepreneur built the house and laid in everything she needed, buying her chickens, a goat and seeds and fencing in the property. When I read the story she had been working with her daughter and little granddaughter for several years to everyone's total satisfaction.

A new world opens up

Out of Russia comes again the hope of the world—famous words by Edgar Cayce the sleeping prophet, and I am very heartened to think that this huge movement now sweeping the world is not only the shape of things to come, but is building up to the critical mass that Jung prophesied would cause the tilt the universe needs to usher in a more peaceful, ethical and loving era.

Have We Lost the Plot?

There is something absolutely fascinating happening in India at present. That's the appearance of the TV guru and in this huge country viewers can choose from a vast number of spiritual channels. Baba Ramdev, the best known, is a yoga guru who is amazingly popular and attracts hundreds of thousands of viewers. Combining yoga, breathing techniques and traditional *ayurvedic* medicine he claims that a range of illnesses can be cured.

The trust he has set up is extremely wealthy and it has financed an ashram, a 300-bed hospital and 1500 *ayurvedic* clinics and centers round India where people are treated free if they have no money, as well as a factory turning out herbal products which are also free to those who cannot pay. Baba Ramdev has become controversial through saying that AIDS, cancer and other diseases, considered as life-threatening in the West, can be cured by such means but I don't think anyone has proved this to be untrue.

The natural approach

Back in 2001 a magnificent film called *Ayurveda — Art of Being* was made and I saw it at the cinema three times. It is available on YouTube and it really is worth an hour or so of anyone's day. It features people suffering from all kinds of illnesses, mental and physical, including cancers, being cured through plants, roots and tree bark as well as minerals of every sort. When the tree bark was tested in a laboratory it was found to kill leukemia cells immediately. Having watched the film yet again I would never say that cancer and AIDS can't be cured by these methods.

Back to the history books

When the British marched into India they endeavored to

suppress the people's ancient beliefs as every occupying force does and people were coerced into taking on the ideas of their masters. *Ayurveda* was outlawed and practitioners who knew which points to press to treat (or cause) paralysis often had their hands or fingers chopped off. Like many nations when under the heel of an oppressor, the people pay lip service and when they obtain their freedom they go back to the way they lived before and *ayurveda* has been around for thousands of years. It is indeed fortunate that the ancient writings were concealed during the occupation and thereby preserved.

A Greek *ayurvedic* practitioner appearing in the film commented that 2000 years ago the *Vedas* gave instructions on how to cure stress and he found it ironic that right now in the West the rates of stress, suicide and alcoholism are higher in doctors than the rest of the population. So the value of *ayurveda* seems to speak for itself. There are now hundreds of books being published in dozens of different languages as well as CD-ROMs and journals, and more and more people are consulting practitioners either in India or in the West for cures which allopathic medicine has failed to offer, and this is where we came in.

Grandma knows best!

Although there is still a widespread belief among the middle classes in India that Western medicine and ideas are best and what has served for thousands of years is just superstition, it seems that many young people are now rediscovering the old methods of healing and a different way of living through the television gurus and that does appear to be a step forward.

Inheritance

Sitting down to a tofu escalope with capers, steamed carrots and broccoli from the organic market not only made me feel hungry but raised a smile. The food I was brought up to eat bears absolutely no resemblance to what I eat today; the past could be a different land. If I'd asked my parents to eat the same thing they would have thought I'd gone mad. For my mother a meat dish was bliss and for my father a meal with any kind of fish was paradise.

Yes, I like fish too, lots of it, although I don't really eat meat of any kind. That isn't to say one is right and the other wrong. The whole point of my musing is the fact that we are not our parents and we need to develop a personality and lifestyle quite apart. This has nothing to do with criticizing them either, because they all do the best they can and mine loved me, which is what matters most.

Although I haven't been ill for more years than I can count, probably partly due to the use of complementary therapies and organic food, I once had to obtain a certificate from a doctor attesting that I was a fit person to work as a complementary therapist and receive patients. That is the law where I live. The doctor asked me about my parents and grandparents, their ailments and their causes of death so that he could build up a picture. I desperately needed that piece of paper so kept my mouth shut about my own ideas. I did a lot of nodding and promising to undertake intrusive and gruesome-sounding tests without any intention of following through.

We are all unique

I only knew my grandmothers and my parents and can say without any judgment on them or me that we are all completely different people. My thought patterns, activities, eating habits are light years away from anything I learnt as a child. The psychosomatic element in any illness fascinates me and I know without the slightest doubt that my life is different and there is absolutely no likelihood that I would suffer from the same illnesses. As I'm a woman the aforementioned doctor naturally asked me about breast cancer in the family and I enjoyed telling him that, yes, my uncle in his 80s had died of breast cancer!

It is interesting when someone comes up with the expression 'My mother suffered from it so I probably will later on' or 'Well, it's in the family'. There is always a greater tendency to something that has affected several members of our families because we have the same genes, but there's no need to sit back, throw up our hands and say there is nothing we can do.

An office colleague died a few years ago at 38 from heart problems. His father and uncle had died around that age and, according to the people who worked beside him, he used to proclaim that he probably wouldn't live beyond 40. Well, he didn't, but his widow and their small children were devastated and had a very hard time coming to terms with losing a young, dynamic husband and father.

We can always change the way we see things and perhaps one of the most important reasons is that when we have absorbed the lessons from those who have gone before and changed our lives in consequence it is unlikely that our future will lie along the same path or that we will end up the same way.

Nature or Nurture?

A colleague of mine has two daughters aged 8 and 4, and a little boy at school with her eldest girl asked her one day: 'Is your daddy your real daddy?'

Puzzled, she replied that he was.

'And is he your sister's daddy too?'

She agreed that he was, although in her class at school that is not the norm.

There are millions of couples all over the world who form a wonderful family unit with their children and who are giving them the tools to build a stable future. There are also millions of men and women who, for one reason or another, are on their own and working miracles to give their children all the love and care they could ever need or want. Let's not forget either extended families who have come together and who have a whole tribe of children as contented as can be with their siblings. Some women have recourse to sperm donors and I know of one or two who are giving the child born as a result a happy and fulfilling life.

Making the best of things

There are unfortunately rather a lot of children who have a different start in life and here I think of someone in my family, a few years older than me. He was born to two people who were completely incompatible and whose married life was a disaster. They divorced and his father married again, raising children who were loved and wanted. What message was that to send to a little boy adrift in the world with his parents using him as a pawn in their pain? We lost touch when I was a teenager but I heard that he married young and was able to enjoy the happy family life he had not known as a child.

I'm not casting stones here because there's a story behind

every family and things happen that we never imagine when we go into the process of making a child with someone.

A poor start but a good finish?

As I believe in synchronicity, a funny thing happened as I was typing this piece. Vivaldi's *Gloria* started to play on my computer which was logged onto a classical music station. Not only do I adore choral music but it immediately took my thoughts to the *Ospedale della Pietà* in Venice where Antonio Vivaldi was the music master for most of his life. The *Ospedale*, which was funded by the Republic and of which there were several in Venice at that time, has been described as an orphanage but that's not quite correct as it didn't only accept orphans. The girls who were sent there were often from extremely well-known and powerful families, even from the nobility, but, because they had been born out of wedlock, as we used to say, they had to be removed from public view.

The aim of the *Ospedale* was to offer an education and practical skills to boys and a musical education to the girls. There were also a few boarders who could pay their way and were gifted musically. Vivaldi, in his time there, turned out dozens of absolutely top-rank musicians and singers and some came to fame in their own right at home and abroad. He composed most of his work in Venice and it was first performed by the girls of the *Ospedale della Pietà*. Vivaldi's music later became unfashionable and he died in poverty, but the legacy he has left us, working with a bunch of outcasts, is absolutely sublime.

So could it be nurture rather than nature that forms our characters? I have met people who have been raised in orphanages and others who have been adopted and who had a wonderfully happy and stable start in life. Difficult starts do not necessarily condemn a child to a painful future, as sometimes they can build on what seems like a great misfortune and often, because they may have to work harder than the rest of us to be accepted, they succeed brilliantly. Here I slip in a mention of Buster Martin who died in 2011, leaving some doubt as to his true age. Suffice to say he was between 97 and 104 and still working three days a week as a van cleaner when he died. He was put into an orphanage at 3 months and thrown out at the age of 10 because he ate too much. He married, raised a family, quickly got bored with retirement and had a long and extremely varied life. Nature rather than nurture in his case seems to have been his *modus vivendi*.

Not Such Ordinary People

Recently I listened to a program on the BBC World Service about men bringing up other men's children.

The first man interviewed had arrived in the UK from Zimbabwe as a refugee and had to wait five years for his wife and two children to join him. He admitted to having had a few affairs at that time. When his wife finally arrived, she, too, had a short-lived affair and became pregnant by another man who rapidly disappeared from her life. Her husband immediately accepted the child, being present at his birth and raising him as his own. He had to put up with discrimination and even hate-messages from his community who felt he had brought shame on them, but he brushed it off and got on with the business of living and bringing up his three children.

Another example was a Welshman who married knowing that his wife was pregnant by another man. He adored the little girl she bore, treating her as his own, and the couple had two more children. When his wife left the family several years later, the children opted to stay with Dad and, although he admitted that things had been hard, they managed. They subsequently entered him in a competition for Father of the Year which he won and, by the time the program was aired, he had married a lady who had two children of her own. With the approval of the whole family she was expecting their baby. The eldest daughter told the inter-viewer how much fun life was with all her brothers and sisters and how she never felt lonely.

Months earlier I heard another story that brought a smile to my face. A couple had married late in life and although it wasn't mentioned whether the man had been married before, his wife had a grown-up daughter with a long-term drug problem. She in her turn had given birth to a son and a daughter, both with slight learning difficulties due to her drug habit. The couple decided to adopt them and give them a home. After only a few years the wife died suddenly, leaving her elderly husband to raise the two children alone. His story was being told as he, too, had also won an award. He explained that, with help, he was able to look after them at home himself and would never let them go simply because: 'I love them to bits,' he explained.

Reaching out

When we talk about a selfish world, what wonderful examples of humanity these are. There must be millions of unsung heroes and heroines around the world, getting on with life, not asking themselves whether they're doing the right thing, not patting themselves on the back for being so charitable.

Even in the direst circumstances people look out for each other. How many heart-warming stories have we read of people who have been in war zones, in prison camps, expecting death at any moment who have reached out to others? For every taker there is a whole army of givers. Would we be able to do that? Impossible to say until we are faced with such a situation, but I truly believe that most of us would come up trumps and that the overwhelming majority of people on this earth are not out to elbow their way to the front but are quietly doing their best. It's this love, respect, thoughtfulness, reaching out—call it what you will—for and to our fellow beings that truly makes life worth living.

Sharing

Paul Theroux, the traveler and writer, in one of his books relates how he passes through Myanmar, spending a few days in Mandalay. There he meets a bicycle rickshaw driver, Oo Nawng, who is a fluent English speaker, having worked as a school teacher until ill-health forced him to retire. He lives in the direst poverty and is frank about the fact that he would probably not live much longer and would be better off dead as, to help him survive, his youngest daughter was forced to work and unable to marry. When Theroux leaves Mandalay for a couple of days he finds he can't get Oo Nawng out of his mind. On the way back he looks out for him and gives him some money with which he can buy a rickshaw instead of renting one and he will be able to pay his rent for a couple of years, too. He doesn't write about it in a 'what a good guy I am' way. He just tells us what he did and probably what many other people who don't write books do as well.

Tithing

Sometimes life seems unfair with a tiny percentage of obscenely rich people getting the goodies while a huge number live on less than a dollar a day. In between there are dozens of levels of have-lesses and have-not-muches, and this question of inequality has caused people over the centuries to try and see how best things can be evened up by sharing. The age-old habit of tithing (giving 10 per cent), which was mentioned in the Bible, has been around for a long time and also applied to tenant farmers who were required to hand over one-tenth of their harvest each year to their landlords. It was paid in the produce they raised as well as the fruits of the trees on their land.

In more recent times tithing has come to mean giving money and has been heavily connected with giving to certain religions;

Judaism, Islam and some forms of Christianity for example. In fact it is a requirement of some religions that adherents tithe 10 per cent of their income. The beneficiaries are supposed to be the poor and needy but that isn't always the case; in some societies it has become just another tax.

The idea has now caught on, but in a different way, in New Age circles; as people worked on their beliefs about money and abundance they came to realize that the more they gave out, the more they tended to receive. Some people stopped there and diligently gave 10 per cent of their income to charities or even to family members going through tough times, feeling that doing something meritorious would lead to getting something back.

Taking it a step further

That's fine, but we can take sharing a step further. Contributing to something we feel is a worthy cause; whether it all goes to one or whether we have several worthy causes doesn't matter. Neither does the sum nor the percentage. We're just stating that we have been very well provided for and we want to share with others who haven't.

There is also the sharing of our time with small organizations that can only function through their volunteers. The array of possibilities is vast and giving a few hours a week to a cause we feel is worthwhile can bring us into the orbit of all kinds of people we would never otherwise meet. For the past few years I have taught English at an evening school, set up and funded for people who can't afford language courses in the private sector (some of the students are refugees, illegals, people on very low wages). The teachers are all volunteers to keep fees to just a token and many amazing people have passed through our doors. When one student asked me what on earth I got out of it, I just had to laugh. What have I got out of it? Probably more than the students themselves will ever know. It has been a totally enriching experience and it reminds me of another example of sharing which is similar in what it achieves.

Reaching out

Prism, an organization I discovered in London a few years ago, collected unwanted books to distribute in prisons. They told me that top of the prisoners' wish lists were self-help books. They had contacted some of the best-known authors in that field and had received parcels of free books to distribute. Perhaps this is one of the greatest forms of sharing; sharing knowledge, on whatever subject. With knowledge you can cover just about everything; it's often only lack of knowledge that keeps people stuck with poor health, in poor homes, in poor jobs. There is an old saying: *Give a man a fish and you feed him for a day; teach him (by sharing your knowledge) to fish and you feed him for a lifetime.*

We, the fortunate ones, have so much to share with our neighbors or with people on the other side of the world. There's no merit in giving what we can't really afford just as there's no shame in feeling good about what little we can do or give; it has to come from the heart. Oh, it isn't the books or the money or our time; it's the desire to share something with someone who has less that warms the heart of the recipient and, by the same token, the giver as well.

The Price of Integrity

I read a novel years ago written by Joe Ashton, a British Labour politician. He insisted that it wasn't based on anyone he knew but its theme was very plausible. The story opened in a mining community in the north of England where the Member of Parliament for 30 years died suddenly of a heart attack, leading to the selection of a new representative. One man who had been active in trade union politics and who had a reputation for helping the underdog was nominated, elected and went to Westminster, happy to be able to make a difference.

Once there he quickly realized that things didn't work that way. The party elders explained that voting was always tactical; sacrificing something they believed in to obtain a bigger prize next time was the order of the day. He was very disillusioned and matters came to a head with the announcement of the closure of an important government-owned facility in his town, throwing hundreds of people out of work. His friends there were confident that he would fight against this iniquity but, once again, he had to toe the party line and vote the way he was told. The story ends with him leaving Westminster to return to his home town where his friends had turned their backs on him.

This was only a novel but the world is full of brave men and women who have stood up for what they consider to be right and spoken out against wrongdoing and cheating.

Amazing courage

Sheila Cassidy was a British doctor who went to work in Chile under the Allende regime. Her duty as she saw it was to treat everyone, regardless of status, and when Augusto Pinochet came to power and she was found to have treated a government opponent who was on the run from the police, she was imprisoned and tortured. She finally returned to the UK where she became a nun for a short period, and then started working in palliative care, later being appointed to direct a hospice for the terminally ill.

Another shining example of integrity was a personal hero of mine. Giovanni Falcone was a Sicilian magistrate who made a career of seeking out and prosecuting Mafia criminals, resulting in a good number being found guilty and imprisoned. He lived as a virtual prisoner himself and was finally murdered, with his wife who was also a magistrate, his bodyguard and chauffeur, by a huge bomb detonated as his car passed over it. He said something very significant when he remarked that if we stay silent and bow our heads we die every time we do so, but the person who speaks out and walks with his head held high only dies once.

Another different kind of price paid for integrity happened a few years ago at the Olympic Games in the finals of a sailing race. A yacht competing in one of the classes capsized and its team got into difficulties. A competitor right up among the leaders, with an excellent chance of being in the medals, turned back and rescued the crew. They obviously missed out on an official medal but they were awarded a special one for their sportsmanship. Participants in these Games have worked and often struggled for years, doing without many things for an opportunity to represent their countries and to benefit from the bounty that brings. To be within touching distance of a medal and then to pass it all up to do what they considered their duty shows real integrity. Such sportsmanship is of course what the Olympic Games should be about.

Could we do that?

The price paid for integrity is invariably very high and many men and women have lost everything, suffered mental and physical torture and even given their lives for what they believe to be right. At the very moment I'm writing this and at the very moment you're reading it, somebody, somewhere is working behind the scenes, at great risk to life and limb, to expose wrongdoing. Those who do live to tell the tale can sleep at night with an easy conscience, knowing they couldn't have done better and that they've given a shining example to the rest of us.

SECTION 5: Belief

A Strange Time of Year

'Christmas' is quite a loaded word because it means so many different things to so many people.

As a child I found it totally magical and I looked forward to it for months before it finally arrived. It was a period when things were hard to get and my family did its best. It was also a time when small was good and the tiniest present was thrilling. It was a time when my parents stayed home from work and when I didn't have to go to bed so early. It was a time when we spent the evening of Christmas Day eating and drinking more than we wanted and playing board games until midnight. In my grandmother's day it was probably an orange and a few nuts in a stocking and slightly better food than they usually ate, but it was surely no less exciting because it was something they didn't have at any other time.

Now, in the part of the world that celebrates it, the whole festivity has become so much less fun. The things that were huge treats in the past would be sniggered at today. People tell of children who take toy catalogues and mark the presents they expect to receive. So where's the magic in that? With very few exceptions I never knew what I was getting, although jigsaw puzzles and books would definitely come into the equation and that was something to look forward to.

As an adult I worked as a listener for the Samaritans in Geneva and then in Brussels and, as I spent my Christmas holidays with my family, was not on duty at that time. My colleagues were swamped with calls and for some periods the team was augmented in order to offer a sympathetic ear to the huge well of pain and loneliness. Statistics tell us there are more relationship break-ups just after the holiday season than at any other time; families who normally see each other occasionally and like it that way are often forced to spend more time than they want together. Having a bit extra to drink loosens tongues and, combined with inactivity and a dose of dyspepsia after the heavy food, you have a recipe for strife.

Change may be on the way

The perfect family with 2.2 children is now in the minority and even many of these families have difficulty in making ends meet, let alone providing all the 'musts' that children want now. The level of shoplifting goes sky high at this time of year and although much of it is the result of greed and taking advantage of crowded shops, some is also perhaps due to people having no other means to give their children the sort of Christmas the media tells them they must have because that's what everyone else is having.

What's happened to our childhood sense of wonder? Our belief in Father Christmas? Our belief in the fact that if we behaved ourselves throughout the year we would be on his calling list? Perhaps being a child at a time when treats really were treats and not something we could have any day of the week made it a real festival of sharing with people we loved and I am so grateful for those wonderful memories.

Christmas is the period when the retail trade expects to max up its takings so the advertising and the merchandising start earlier and earlier, almost as soon as the summer holidays are over. As things seem to go round in circles, perhaps we are nearly at the end of the consumer boom and ready to get back to a more sober celebration of the season, one that doesn't mean a ten-day orgy of spending money we don't have and overeating and drinking to the detriment of our livers. I really hope so.

Beliefs

I don't know whether William Shakespeare really wrote the works he was said to have written but, in my opinion, whoever did was a genius and a quote from *Hamlet* that I like very much is this:

> *There are more things in heaven and earth, Horatio,*
> *Than are dreamt of in your philosophy*

So often, it turns out to be true.

The White Queen in *Alice in Wonderland* had another way of looking at beliefs when she said: 'Why, sometimes I've believed as many as six impossible things before breakfast.'

And yet we're all (and I include myself) stuck in our belief systems and although as we grow to adulthood we shake off a lot of the beliefs of the people who raised us and educated us, it is not all that common to decide to do things in a very different way or to step out of the slot in life that we have been conditioned to fill.

Beliefs can be changed

We have been taught that eating, and especially drinking loads of water, is absolutely essential to keep us alive, but there are people in the world who haven't eaten and some who haven't drunk either for many years. For example, there is an Indian guru who, not having eaten or drunk for 40 years, was subjected to a whole battery of tests in a high-tech hospital in India. The specialists could find absolutely no explanation for the phenomenon so another belief hits the dust.

There is also the case of yogi in the Himalayas and many people have seen this for themselves. They sit in sub-zero temperatures with their naked bodies wrapped in sheets that have been soaked in cold water and within a very short time steam rises as they control their bodily heat and dry out the sheets. Totally impossible, we might say, but far too many people have witnessed it for us to refuse to believe it.

However, when it comes to religious or cultural beliefs we can be inclined to stay in the mold of our background, although we can travel widely or live abroad. We may not even consider that other people have a right to believe in something different and many wars or acts of genocide over the millennia have been caused by one set of people endeavoring to impose its beliefs on another; the fear of the other whose beliefs we don't share which make him different, alien, above all dangerous, to be annihilated at whatever cost.

How we tend to categorize

We split people up into artificial groups based on religion, class, color, nationality, appearance and goodness knows what else. Let's take appearance, because I've often fallen into this trap, although, to use an old-fashioned expression, you shouldn't judge a book by its cover. For example, a lady whom I knew slightly is always dressed from head to foot in black. She's Italian, a classic example of a Sicilian Catholic peasant you may say — and I did. Well, no, when I got to know her better I discovered that she's from a major city in mainland Italy, wears black because it's her favorite color, has a good job, two daughters whose studies have landed them interesting careers and she's a practicing Protestant.

When I lived in Scotland young people asked each other what school they had gone to. This told them whether the person was from the Catholic or Protestant side of the religious divide and whether they had any future as friends. In England where I grew up the question was 'What does your father do?' That gave a good idea of the class pigeonhole into which we could put the person. As a child, if the first representative I met of any particular nationality was doing a very menial job or smelt of something exotic or looked unkempt or dirty or was untrustworthy, I put that whole nation in the same bag and it is from these first impressions that our view of the world is formed.

Two women I know were recently criticizing the youth of today and how hellish to have to teach them. One is a teacher, but my experience with young people is a great deal vaster than that of the other person. I've found that those I meet or teach, or the sons and daughters of friends, are far more mature than I was at their age and are actually exceptional human beings. The beliefs of those other women are certainly not universally shared.

Beliefs can be changed

Again there are young people and those not so young who, often through their families' belief systems, are convinced they can only be happy if they get their hands on everything they want as fast as possible, whether it already belongs to someone else or not.

Life's circumstances can forge our beliefs. A friend living in an apartment block told of putting her shopping down to check her mailbox. She heard a sound and, turning round, saw a small girl in the process of stealing her bag. It was at a time when refugees from former Yugoslavia were arriving in Western Europe. It isn't surprising that the child's belief about food, and whether she was going to find any to eat or not, led her to grab what she could when she could; her life up to that point had probably been a struggle for survival.

It is important to be flexible in our beliefs about other people and things because they can be changed. Nothing is written in stone; nothing is real. When we are able to do just that—and sometimes it's as hard as turning an ocean-going tanker—life changes immeasurably and we are invariably better for it.

Comfort Zones

The amazing Helen Keller, born with serious handicaps, considered that life was either an amazing adventure or worth nothing at all and these words are a constant source of inspiration for us to leave our comfort zones and reach out for something better, although we certainly need faith and courage to get there. The fact that her words are so often quoted leads me to believe that people are crying out for such messages.

Somebody once said that ships are safest when they're in port, but that ships are designed to leave their ports and sail far and wide, and it's probably the best description of comfort zones I know.

Physically speaking, a comfort zone is reckoned to be around 23 degrees Celsius, not too hot and not too cold. It's pleasant to be there, but after a while we long for something different. Several years ago when I lived in Marseille in southern France from January to April, we had sun every day and although it was often cold (just spend 15 days with the *mistral* blowing full force and you'll never forget it) it never rained. And I missed the rain!

Similarly in our lives we can find ourselves in a position where we're neither happy nor really unhappy but we don't want to rock the boat by trying something that could change things into something we expect to be worse. Some bright spark once said that the only thing more stressful than change is the absence of change.

Now why should that be? We all have our own idea, but mine is that we are not here to vegetate, to choose the easy option, especially if it doesn't make us joyful. At the age of 90, Charles Fillimore, one of the founders of the Unity movement, said that every morning he jumped out of bed fizzing with excitement about what the day might bring.

Going beyond

I've had dozens of different jobs in my life but one of the most tedious was working in a café. We took it in turns either doing the washing-up and preparing the salads or serving the clients and, apart from changing our duties every other day, we knew in advance right down to the content of our conversations with customers how the time would be spent. It was a comfort zone for me at that time because it was the only means I had of earning a living but when I got fired after a few months it was a blessing to have someone else make up my mind for me.

We can look back to the teenagers of the 1960s who started to pick out tunes on a guitar, or learnt to play the drums or could sing, and who practiced in their bedrooms and trailed round to tiny gigs to play their music. Plenty of them gave up studies and jobs to become full-time musicians, often to the disapproval of their parents. They arrived on the scene at the exact moment that pop music as we know it was exploding all over the world and, 50 years later, many of them are still performing, touring the world, playing to huge audiences, living the life they couldn't ever have imagined when they started out.

They've had their ups and downs of course and have needed to develop thick skins to ward off some of the criticism to which they've been subjected, but when you're doing something you love and you know you're doing it superbly, the opinions of a few sour people really don't matter much.

When it all works out

I had a friend a long time ago who absolutely adored what he did—his career and his comfort zone had converged. He was passionate about the theater and, on leaving school, he chose to study engineering at a university known for the quality of its amateur theater club. He immediately became a member and once he had graduated, everything else was left behind as he pursued his overriding interest. When I knew him, not only was theater lighting his job, but in his spare time he did the lighting for the plays put on by the local university and he attended every single theatrical performance in the city where we worked. He lived and breathed theater; it was his whole life.

This then must be the ultimate comfort zone/life path/passion. How many of us find it? Unless we do what we love, unless we love what we do, unless we follow our dreams, there are probably not many of us in that delightful position.

It's All in the Mind

A student in my English class bemoaned the fact that she had trouble remembering the things she learnt each week and put it sorrowfully down to age although she's not that old. I stopped her right there. Unless we have some kind of advancing senility (which she hasn't) there is nothing wrong with our minds. What I'm convinced does happen is that when we're younger we have less information and fewer things to think about. As we age, we develop all manner of ideas, learn more things and how to do them and become a veritable scrapbook of information.

Nothing wrong with that but it makes it much harder to find the file we need each time we open our mental drawer. It's also true that we hear and are obliged to learn things that may not interest us in the slightest and these can be hard to grasp and hold on to. We may have a vague recollection of the information but no more and certainly not enough to come to the fore when we next try to access it. I have noticed that when I need to know something about the workings of my computer or grammar rules for teaching English for example, I have to write them down otherwise they go in one ear and out the other. When I was learning French I used to work hard on some of the less-used tenses and vocabulary every single time I had an exam to pass and once that was over the material receded back into the shadows, having to be brought out and relearnt for the next time.

When we need the information

Trying to understand how the tax system works, I had it all explained to me on two separate occasions by a long-suffering friend. As she was telling me, it all made complete sense and I really cottoned on: ten minutes later it had been totally wiped from my memory. Very frustrating, but as my life doesn't depend on learning about it I have settled for not knowing.

When it comes to the things that I'm passionate about, the information is readily available. Giving a talk on a subject dear to me is no real hassle because I almost feel as if I'm channeling; ideas I didn't know I had and that fit perfectly into the context spring to mind. I love giving examples to illustrate my point, because that's the way I retain information, and they seem to leap unbidden into my head. When I'm writing an article the same thing happens: I choose a subject and suddenly what I thought of as a long-forgotten anecdote comes rushing to the forefront of my mind to illustrate my point.

Sometimes information we need urgently leaps to the surface and we have no idea where it came from. How many times have we heard stories of people in mortal danger when a passer-by, without knowing how s/he knew, was able to administer a life-saving technique?

Or babies born, for example, in the back of a taxi before the mother arrived at the hospital? The people who've rushed in to help may not know how it was they knew what to do. Sometimes it's not even something they've done before, but a sort of instinct seems to click in and has taken over, guiding their hands and their brains.

So it doesn't really matter if my student can't remember how to use a modal verb; when she absolutely needs to dredge some vital piece of information up from the hidden recesses of her mind, something she thought she had forgotten or something she didn't think she'd ever learnt, when her life or someone else's may be depending on it, it won't fail her.

Jane's Story

Attending a conference in the magical center at Asilomar on the Pacific coast near Monterey, California a few years back, I was waiting in line for the restaurant to open on the first evening when I heard a lady behind me chatting to someone and saying: 'Oh yes, I intended to make a lot of money and I had a great time doing it.'

Intriguing! She sounded like someone I'd like to meet. That evening, although we sat at the same table, there were a lot of other people around us and it was only at the end of the week that she told me her story.

A middle-aged woman, newly divorced, Jane had visited a tiny rural town in Arizona and decided that was where she wanted to live. Her children were scathing: a 'What on earth will you do in a backwater like that?' type of scathing. It was a very, very small place in those days.

Making it happen

But Jane had fallen in love with the area at first sight. She knew it was where she was meant to be so she went ahead, rented somewhere to live and looked for a job. She found an advertisement for a receptionist/assistant with a local real estate agent, made an appointment and turned up for an interview. While she was sitting in the waiting room, in came another candidate, a much younger and extremely glamorous woman.

'Aha,' thought Jane, 'what can I do about this?'

She was called in first and after the preliminaries she put it to the head of the agency and this is how she did it.

'If you want someone to look good when clients come in, if you want someone who's young and beautifully turned out, hire the girl in the waiting room. On the other hand, if you want someone who's prepared to turn her hand to anything, someone who is never ill, who will work round the clock and who will go out of her way to help your clients, then hire me.'

There was of course no contest and fortunately the interviewer saw her point, offering her the job immediately.

Over the years, the town and the surrounding area grew from being a backwater to a small city and Jane's boss paid for her to attend courses to become a real estate agent herself. When I met her she was around 70 and she told me she still helped out now and then, showing clients round properties. One of them had recently told her: 'You're so good at this you should be doing it full time.'

'Oh no,' she replied, 'I *have* done it full time, made plenty of money and had a wonderful life.'

Listening to Our Intuition

It's not only when we are quiet and peaceful that we hear that still small voice. Of course it can be then, but our intuition speaks to us all the time and in many ways.

Once when I was trying to plan a trip to the USA with a friend for whom it would be a first visit, we got stuck. We had decided go to the Southwest and tour some of the national parks—my favorite places. Our plan was to stay for three weeks and my friend was still unsure about whether or not she would like the desert despite my efforts to explain that it wasn't exactly the Sahara. I was spending a weekend with her to plan our final itinerary and choose our flights, but on the day I was due to go home we were no further forward. It was early spring and unseasonably warm. While she went to prepare lunch I sat on the balcony and soaked up the sun, letting my mind wander. Suddenly the words 'San Francisco' flashed up in front of my eyes. I leapt up, dashed into the kitchen and put it to her: 'If we spent a week in San Francisco, what do you think?'

She loved the idea and that's what we did. With great success.

Dreams have messages for us

Another example was the result of a dream. I had planned to go with a group to India to visit some ashrams. The trip was expensive and I had to pay over half the money up front. As I received more and more information from the organizer I began to go off the idea big time. I still don't know why; the difficulty of getting a visa may have come into the equation but it was the uncomfortable feeling that bothered me. Then I had a dream, a very clear dream in which I saw the words: 'Don't trust the people you're going with.' I knew what it referred to and, although I had already put down nearly £1000 as a deposit, the next day I sent a fax canceling everything and felt an immediate sense of relief.

A very amusing instance of using my intuition happened when I was living in Totnes, a village in the heart of South Devon down in the south-west corner of the UK. Getting rapidly bored with village life I was stuck about what to do next. One evening I was driving to an event in Torquay, a town a few miles away, chatting out loud to myself, asking where I was supposed to go. As in all the best conversations, I answered my own questions, telling myself that if we knew everything in advance what would be the point in life?

'No, but just a sign would be really helpful,' I countered.

Well, I didn't wait long. A few miles further on I came to a T junction where I needed to turn left and the signpost read 'Exeter'. (Exeter is the largest city in the area.)

'Aha,' I thought, 'that's where I'll go next.' So I did.

This is certainly not to say that I'm an absolute whizz at listening to messages and getting it right. The fact that I remember these occurrences is simply because they were moments when the question was clear and the answer too, but if I'd made a different decision or not even noticed that feeling of YES when we know we've got it right, then I'm sure something else would have turned up to send me off in a different direction.

Not Your Time

After reading Raymond Moody's seminal book *Life After Life* I became very interested in near-death experiences. These are events recounted by people who have been pronounced clinically dead but, sometimes against all the odds, have returned to life and told astonishingly similar stories of their experiences in the afterlife. One thing most of them mention is seeing a relative or a friend whom they know to be dead and whom either they can't physically reach or who tells them: 'Go back; it's not your time.'

A brush with death

We are all familiar with stories of spectacular brushes with death when there is a major accident. Tales of airline employees who have changed shifts at the last minute such as the stewardess who was doing a friend a favor by taking her place or the steward caught in a traffic jam on the way to the airport, arriving too late for his flight and its subsequent crash, are told practically every time there is an aviation disaster.

People who adhere to a particular religion see the divine hand of providence at work here, but for me it means that the person in question has a lot more to do before dying and many people have gone on to look at life in a completely different way because they have lost any fear they had about death.

Some wonderful tales

There are some amazing examples to illustrate the fact that it is not the right time to die, but among my favorites is the story of a church in Beatrice, Nebraska which held its choir practice once a week, with the 15 members arriving at 7.15pm to start at 7.20pm sharp. Although they were always ready to start on time, on one particular evening back in the 1950s everyone was late: the minister was finishing his sermon, one member was listening to the end of a radio program, one didn't realize his watch was slow, another had dropped off to sleep, someone else was finishing the laundry, two women's cars refused to start, and so on. This meant that when the boiler exploded, demolishing the church at 7.27pm, the time when choir practice was normally in full swing, nobody had yet turned up.

Another story I have read in several places is about a man who worked in a large building and needed to take the lift down to go to lunch. When the lift arrived there was room for him, but a vague feeling that something wasn't quite right caused him to hesitate so he let it go. When the doors closed, the cable broke and the lift crashed to the bottom of the shaft, causing death and injury to the occupants.

Personal experience

The fact that it wasn't my time was brought home to me in 1984 when the Liverpool and Juventus soccer teams were playing in the European Cup final at the Heysel Stadium in Brussels. I lived in Belgium at that time and my partner who was Italian and, like many Italians, a football fanatic, had bought tickets for us to attend. I, too, loved football and was excited at the thought of going; although as an afterthought, he decided that with the English fans' reputation for violence it wasn't safe to take me. He decided not to give the tickets to his teenage son for the same reason and he finally sold them to an acquaintance whom he saw again the day after the match. He had an arm in plaster and had returned home alone, his friend having died at the stadium.

In such circumstances a lot has been written about survivor guilt; some people spend long years in therapy and some never get over the thought that dozens died but they were spared. When one of the dead was someone close, of course there is the normal grief of loss as well. If, though, you can see as we did, that it just wasn't our time, it spurs you to greater efforts to find your life path and accomplish your mission while you have the opportunity.

Premonitions and Precognition

Larry Dossey, a Texan medical doctor who is fascinated by the role of the mind in illness, has written many works on the subject.

I have been listening to him read *The Power of Premonitions: How Knowing the Future Can Shape Our Lives* and have found it fascinating. In Dossey's opinion, premonitions and precognition amount to the same thing: a knowing about an event before it happens, although I am not so sure. To my mind, a premonition is a *feeling* of unspecified doom or disaster (less often something positive) and precognition is *living* or *seeing* something that hasn't happened yet.

Dossey gives many examples of both in spectacular disasters such as in the Welsh town of Aberfan in 1966 when a mountain of coal waste engulfed a school, killing most of the children, after several people had had visions of piles of wet mud crashing down on a building in dreams, or the events in the USA in 2001 when people had premonitory dreams of plane crashes and buildings on fire. Nobody in either case had sufficient concrete evidence to alert the authorities and who would have listened anyway?

The scientific experiments

As you would imagine, thousands of scientific experiments have been carried out into all aspects of forecasting or foreknowing and, studying the monetary aspect, Dossey has been able to conclude that aiming just to get very rich through forecasting the future doesn't work. Pure greed seems to rule out success when a person is working solely to make lots of money, and he has plenty of stories to illustrate this.

Need is a different matter and he tells of a lady who needed to repair her roof and just didn't have the money. She prayed for the sum required and dreamt of lottery numbers. Using them, she won the exact amount. Three years later, once more in financial straits, she asked again, and again she dreamt of lottery numbers which delivered to her the precise sum she wanted.

He also tells of an experiment carried out with Beverly Jaegers, a psychic from St. Louis, Missouri, who had phenomenal success later on with remote viewing—training oneself to see something at a distance—teaching the skill to police officers who were able to locate bodies, solve crimes, etc. Ms. Jaegers was asked to predict the future of a handful of investments and was pitted against the experts. One did slightly better in his informed predictions but she beat the others hands down.

Pete Dixon, a commodities broker in the 1970s, wanted to know about the future of coffee prices. He gave Ms. Jaegers a sealed envelope with a note inside saying coffee prices were going to rise. He promised her that if he made money he would buy her a new house. Taking the envelope in her hands, she told him she was seeing heavy rain in Brazil and people with baskets with a few red berries in them. Against all the odds, Dixon bought heavily and, when coffee prices shot up as a result of unseasonably bad weather in Brazil, he made a fortune, and, honoring his promise to Ms. Jaegers, gave her the money to buy a new house.

A glimpse of the future

Some of the most mind-blowing reports show that events have been known about before they have happened; which should be absolutely impossible but which does take us into the realm of quantum physics. Reg Presley, the lead singer in The Troggs, a well-known pop group in the UK in the 1960s, is fascinated by *Wild Things They Don't Tell Us* which is the title of a book he has written. In it he mentions being at home one day and watching the lunchtime news on television. He saw a huge conflagration at a chemical plant which was melting windows half a mile away.

So impressed was he with the heat needed to be generated to do that, he told his wife about it when she returned from shopping in the middle of the afternoon.

While watching the evening news, he called her to come and see. It was reported that a huge fire had broken out in a chemical plant at Flixborough in the UK at 4.45 in the afternoon. The cameras then went direct to Flixborough where to his utter amazement he watched the same report he had seen six hours earlier. His wife turned to him, asking him: 'How could you have seen that before it happened?' All he could say was that he had.

The *Titanic*—the most famous example

Possibly the most reported instance of precognition involved the sinking of the *Titanic*. In 1898, Morgan Robertson, a little-known writer, produced a novelette about a ship called the *Titan* that sank after hitting an iceberg on its way to New York, trying to break a speed record, just like the *Titanic* 14 years later. He wrote about insufficient lifeboats for all those aboard and talked about certain features which had never been seen on a ship until they were built into the *Titanic* in 1912.

In 1909, in a book entitled *Beyond the Spectrum*, Robertson wrote about submarines replacing battleships, and land battles replacing sea battles; all of which came to pass several years later during the First World War. He also wrote about a war breaking out between the USA and Japan, started by a surprise Japanese attack on US naval vessels, foreshadowing the attack on Pearl Harbor in 1941. Today he is largely forgotten and I was astonished that when talking about the premonitions of people who canceled their trips on the *Titanic*, not even a mention was made of Morgan Robertson in Dossey's comprehensive and fascinating study, although for me his name will be forever linked to that ill-starred liner.

Acting on our dreams

When having a vivid dream or a feeling about something, we can dismiss it or, if we tell anyone about it, we can likely hear that it's nothing more than a bad dream or wishful thinking or any manner of things. Of course we don't always go with the feeling and sometimes it is too fantastic or incomplete to be of any use. What is striking is that when the dreamer is not personally involved, the information seems to be vague and would be of little use to anyone; when the person is directly involved then sufficient information is often given for him or her to avoid a tragic outcome if it is believed and followed. This is a truly fascinating field of study and the Rhine Research Center in the USA has gone probably as far as anyone in research into human consciousness. Should the notion anchor itself in our belief systems, what a different world we would inhabit.

Shyness

One evening my English class was struggling with adjectives and their opposites. We were working on a text where the students had to put them in the relevant columns, with a column for any adjectives that could be negative or positive. One of the words that could be either was 'shy' and, the next day, seeing a man on a bicycle riding past on the pavement took me back to an occasion where being shy got me into a load of trouble.

And I still remember it

I was around 9 or 10 at the time and my mother and I did a lot of cycling. One morning during the school holidays we were on our way home and we stopped at a local parade of shops for her to pick up something. I was left in charge of her bike propped against the wall. A man came out on his way to lunch, jumped on my mother's bike and pedaled off up the road. I was completely paralyzed. Far too shy and embarrassed to say anything to a grown-up I didn't know or even one I *did* know, I could only watch aghast as he disappeared into the distance, wondering how on earth I was going to explain that away.

When my mother arrived and found the bike missing, I tried to tell her I had been looking at something else and hadn't seen anyone take it but she was justifiably angry and I went straight to my bedroom when we got home while she phoned the shop. Apparently the man had gone to work on his wife's bike that morning and when he got home and discovered that it was the wrong one he had contacted the shop immediately, so Mum was much mollified and I was allowed to come downstairs. I laugh about it now, but 'shy' in that context would definitely have gone into the column of negatives.

Many years later when I'd got over my shyness to a certain extent, I had a good friend who was quite the opposite. We had a mutual friend who had worked with her mother at one time and she told me that Michelle was most unpopular with her mother's colleagues because she was so pushy and full of herself. Basically a decent and generous girl, a modicum of shyness would have been a very positive attribute in her relationships with other people.

Judging the situation

So where to draw the line? If we can judge the temperature of the situation, it's easy to be a little retiring or, if there's a need to speak our mind, then we must. Sometimes that's hard for me, and my shyness and a fear of speaking my mind lead me to keep quiet when I should say something until one day, pushed beyond the limit, out comes a whole stream of reproaches that I've tried to keep under wraps. A very negative aspect of shyness.

I admire my oldest friend here because she says what's on her mind when it arises, and because there is something so innately clear and honest about her, everyone knows where they stand. She has lectured me now and then, usually about my failure to stand up for myself, and when I've thought about her words, which have invariably stung at the time, they have been a great help in the long run. She's probably not really shy but she's definitely not pushy either. Even after so many years of knowing her, I envy the way she handles situations. She would certainly qualify for the column marked 'both' or, if you prefer, 'neither'.

The Intelligence of Animals

Taking a stroll along an unfamiliar footpath one Sunday afternoon, I came to a fork with no indication as to where either path led. A middle-aged lady with a fox terrier stopped and explained the options. We carried on chatting and I decided to walk with her and her dog and, as her home was nearby, she invited me to stop for tea on the way back.

People don't usually invite perfect strangers into their homes for tea and I commented on it as she served me a slice of home-made cake. She laughed and pointed to her dog who was chilling out on the floor beside us after his walk. She explained that a workman had recently been sent to repair a radiator and the dog wouldn't stop growling at him. She'd asked the company not to send him again as she trusted implicitly her dog's judgment.

A finely tuned instinct

Animal instinct is absolutely brilliant, far better attuned than ours, and possibly the very best demonstration of it is from a report about the Asian tsunami in 2004. Around 20 minutes before it struck, several elephants were returning to Phuket after taking tourists on a trip. Five of them were already tethered but the four who were still at large managed to drag their companions free and they rapidly climbed to higher ground. Realizing that something was happening, local people started following them and were thereby saved when the wave broke.

What was really touching was that immediately after the water had receded the elephants charged down and began picking up children with their trunks, taking them to a place of safety. When all the children had been rescued they started picking up the adults. They saved 42 people and then collected four dead bodies, not allowing their handlers to mount them until the work was finished. Then they started gathering debris.

They know we're on our way home

What an amazing lesson for us, although one person who wouldn't have been in the least surprised is Rupert Sheldrake, the illustrious biologist who first brought the theory of morphic resonance to our attention and who is the author of a book with an imposing title: *Dogs That Know When Their Owners Are Coming Home: And Other Unexplained Powers of Animals*. In many cases he found that an animal would sit at the door to wait for its owner, even at a time s/he didn't usually come home, and it was never wrong.

Our cat, Mickey, certainly knew when my mother was coming home as, every day, he sat at the window at the appointed time to watch for her. When her car drew up he demanded to be let out and would shoot off to the garage at the end of the garden.

The routine was always the same and my mother scrupulously followed it; getting out of the car to open the garage doors she would pet him as he rolled on the ground. When he had had enough he would jump up and stand back until the car was inside and the doors shut. He then allowed himself to be picked up and carried halfway up the path, always struggling to get down at the same point and heading the procession to the door.

Bob the street cat

As you can imagine, for a cat lover, when my eye caught a piercingly intelligent gaze staring out at me from the cover of a book in a local shop I just had to investigate further. *A Street Cat Named Bob* was written by the cat's companion James Bowen and is a magnificent story of hope and unconditional love. In Bowen's own words: 'he's a very special little man.'

Bowen, a street musician in London, recovering from a heroin habit and living from hand to mouth in sheltered accommodation, met a stray cat one evening in the entrance to his apartment block. He took him in and attended to his wounds, spending his last few bits of money on antibiotics and food for him. He nursed the cat he called 'Bob' back to health and then tried to set him loose on the street where he felt he belonged. Bob had completely different ideas and stuck to his new friend like glue.

He loved going everywhere with Bowen, walking down the street on his lead, sitting on a bus watching life go by or wrapped round Bowen's neck and as more and more people stopped to pet him, the money rolled in faster, leading to jealousy from certain quarters; street people are in survival mode and nobody wants to see someone else doing better. Going somewhere new or doing something different, Bob would stop, cast a quizzical glance at Bowen, see that it was OK and carry on walking.

As time went by, the bond between them strengthened and their roles reversed with Bob 'nursing' Bowen back to health, as he got off his heroin substitute and took up the responsibility of having two mouths to feed. One little anecdote from the book that illustrates what kind of cat Bob is: he was snoozing (like most cats, with one eye open) at Bowen's feet one day when a Staffordshire terrier was drawn to his biscuits in a bowl on the ground. He was moving in to investigate further when Bob jumped up, gave him a slap on the nose and the dog, thrown off balance, immediately began to backpedal and was dragged away by his owner with his tail down. Satisfied with his defense of his territory, Bob settled back to sleep.

Bob is now world famous, with videos on YouTube, and people come from every corner of the globe to meet him as he and his companion sit outside the Angel underground station (yes, the synchronicity of the name wasn't lost on me; it seems that someone has really been watching over the two friends) selling the street magazine *The Big Issue*.

This not only illustrates the intelligence of animals but is a truly awesome example of unconditional love. We often think of parents unconditionally loving their children but it's not always the case. In our own lives, how many of us manage friendships and relationships where we are so unconditional in our feelings? Where all we want to do is give and give regardless of what, if anything, we'll get back?

People who have no contact with animals rarely pay any attention to their behavior. That is their loss because animal intuition seems to be much more developed than ours, probably as a result of their inbred survival instincts. As Bob demonstrates, they have much to teach us about caring, fidelity and some of the better qualities in life that many of us may have forgotten.

The Power of Love

It's a sobering thought really; when we consider that every other being in this world is connected to us and is literally part of us. Wayne Dyer, author and workshop leader, tells about a time one of his children was a baby. He and his wife were out shopping when she told him the baby was hungry and she needed to go home and feed him. When he asked her how she knew, she informed him her milk had come in. In the same way how do some people know when a loved one is in distress or wake at night and know they are having a visit from someone who has just come to say goodbye before leaving the earth plane?

Deepak Chopra has written about a laboratory where rabbits were kept for research into new drugs. They were put into batches and each batch had its own handler. The researchers were puzzled by the fact that the drugs, which killed off and caused suffering to the majority of the rabbits, had no effect on one particular batch. They looked more closely and found that the girl caring for them always stroked them as she put them back into their cages. The power of love, of caring, was negating the damage caused by the drugs.

Love is amazing

We have heard that love can move mountains and there have been many stories of children facing certain death coming back to live a normal life through the faith of their parents and the prayers of the people around them. There have also been stories of people managing superhuman physical feats when the life of a loved one is in danger, the kind of things they could never normally do.

I once knew an elderly lady who was crippled with arthritis and would lie awake at night in agony. One evening, when her grandson had collapsed on the floor, she was on her knees in a flash giving him mouth-to-mouth resuscitation. Normally there was absolutely no way she could ever have managed to kneel on the floor but through her love for him she didn't have time to think about whether or not she could.

Tony Stockwell, a well-known British medium and healer, tells of a small charity which sponsors young Buddhist monks living in exile in India. The charity seeks people to fund a monk and enable him to complete his studies, and the exchange of letters between the sponsor and the sponsored becomes a rich source of sharing. The friend who had introduced Stockwell to the charity was diagnosed with a form of cancer for which the prognosis wasn't at all optimistic. She wrote about it to her sponsored monk. To her amazement the tumor began to shrink and her prognosis became far less dismal. She told the monk, who explained that when he received the news, the whole monastery had started regularly chanting and praying for her well-being. The lady had no doubt whatsoever that this was the reason she was regaining her health.

The power of prayer can also be construed as love; if we didn't have a feeling of love or empathy with the person being prayed for, we wouldn't be doing it. I don't necessarily mean prayer as we think of it here either; it can take many forms and just having a loving thought for someone or wishing them well in our minds can constitute a prayer.

Love in action

Near to where I live there is a house which was the home of a couple who worked with flowers, making up pretty bunches and bouquets. They always had a table outside with several bunches at various prices and the money was to be put in a slot in the front door. The lady is now elderly and a widow and the flowers are her pride and joy. She told me that people didn't always pay for what they took but she wanted to keep on as long as she could. What is extraordinary (although on second thoughts, perhaps it's not) is that the flowers I buy from her live much longer than those from anywhere else. I guess it's because she puts her heart into what she does.

The energy of love is extremely powerful and we should never underestimate its benefits. It only takes a second to send a loving thought to someone, anyone, who may be in need of it but it can change a life—perhaps ours as well as theirs.

This Too Will Pass

Pamela Harriman led an extremely colorful life. Born into a rich and titled family, she married Randolph Churchill, the son of Sir Winston Churchill, at the age of 19. Her father-in-law immediately saw her potential as a mover and shaker and she excelled at just that for the rest of her life. Her marriages and multiple liaisons with rich, famous and powerful men were the stuff of gossip columns and would be considered scandalous even today. She ended her career as US ambassador to France under the Clinton administration, dying after suffering a cerebral hemorrhage in the Embassy's swimming pool.

She knew not only the good times, but some very unhappy and difficult times too. She had to suffer being rejected and ostracized for her notoriety and when you have been fêted by presidents and famous people that's hard to take. At one time she fled Paris for the USA where few people knew about her past and there she stayed, marrying two well-connected and elderly millionaires, both of whom she outlived. Despite everything, whenever she received another setback, one of her favorite sayings was: *This too will pass,* and I can't help feeling how right she was.

Nothing lasts forever

Of course it's great to know that a tragedy, a bereavement, the loss of a job, an illness, even a bout of indigestion will pass, but we must also come to terms with the fact that good, wonderful, heart-soaring events will also pass. They would be less blissful if they never stopped and we would doubtless downgrade them from 'wonderful, heart-soaring' to something like 'very pleasant' or, worse, we might not notice them at all and just take them for granted.

Life's roller coaster, on which we've all embarked, is part of the human condition and without the dark we would never appreciate the light. There's polarity in everything and a diet purely of ice cream (or if you prefer it, chocolate) would quickly pall, just as one disaster after another could cause us to capsize.

The saying *What doesn't kill you makes you stronger* could have been written for people like Pamela Harriman and if we look back at our lives, at some of the really tough times, we can see how they have made us more resilient. Developing a 'been there, done that, got the T-shirt' attitude is really helpful. One thing is vital: we must learn from the challenges thrown in our faces by deciding to try doing things a different way next time or, if it's something outside our control, to understand that if we came through the first time, we're likely to come through a second time. These are the true growth periods in our lives and we need them in order to go on to bigger and better things.

Staying in the moment

We must also learn to love wholly and passionately the good times by living them in the moment and not fretting about what will happen when they've gone. We will then have proved to ourselves that, good or bad, that too has passed. Something important has been learnt and, although we might come out of it bruised and battered, we're stronger and wiser and have lived to tell the tale.

Thoughts Are Things

Thoughts are things is a quote used by Ernest Holmes, the founder of Science of Mind, although he may not have been the originator, and many other people over the years have proved that it works.

To illustrate the point, spending a weekend in London, I watched a program about a small town in the north of England which had a statue of a dog in its local park with a reputation for bringing good luck to those who patted its head. The presenter decided to test this and a group of people who were willing to have a go was selected. One of them, a butcher called Wayne, laughingly informed him that he never had any good luck anyway and he didn't expect any change after patting the dog. At the end of the first week he could even report yet another mishap that had befallen him.

Everyone else who took part was thrilled with the results as they reported success with finding employment, winning raffles and bonus ball competitions, etc. After one patting visit, a local pub landlady was delighted to be offered a free gig by a well-known local comedian and as the tale of the dog has become known, more and more people come from far and near to pat him.

So how did Wayne get on? Well, his series of mishaps and disasters continued and the TV crew tried various ways to get him to look on the bright side. They even dropped a £50 note on the path he normally took to work. To no avail as he walked right past it. They eventually made up a huge mobile billboard reading: 'If your name is Wayne, please call this number', driving it slowly past him on his way to his shop. He did notice that!

The moral of the story

So what is the moral of the story? Well, as its title suggests: thoughts are things. If people believe in a thing wholeheartedly it tends to happen, but how many of us are like Wayne and don't even notice something good when it's right under our noses? If not so glass-half-empty as Wayne, do we always notice the little signs telling us that change is on the way and we're not forgotten in the great scheme of things? The positive thinkers, who always expect the best whatever happens, tend to get just that, and those who believe that nothing good ever happens to them seem convinced that life's out to get them.

Going back to the dog, there's something else at work here, and not only because people believed that patting its head would bring them luck. The positive energy built up by the believers in that spot became more available to everyone who visited it and this is how certain power centers may have gained their reputations.

We make our own luck through our personal belief systems, but this can be so much stronger when we link into the positive thoughts of all those who have preceded us and who have expected only good outcomes. Here's another quote, possibly also from Ernest Holmes that bears thinking about: *What you believe is.*

Henry Ford, apart from being a highly successful car manufacturer, had a reputation for being a bit of a philosopher and one of his most quoted truisms was that whether we believe we can or whether we believe we can't, we're right in both instances. His sentiments accord with so many others'. So let's discipline ourselves to think only of good outcomes and we certainly won't be disappointed.

Through the Eyes of a Child

There are one or two people who have created small master-pieces. Of course everyone has his or her own favorites, but these particular stories inspire me time and again.

The Little Prince is the sort of work you can say is written for children but which has so many lessons to offer to the adult reader. On his travels to Planet Earth, the little Prince meets many different characters: the king who has no subjects; the vain man with nobody to admire him; the drunkard who drinks to forget the shame of being a drunkard; the businessman who seeks things like the stars to count so that he can possess them; the lamplighter whose planet turns so fast he needs to light and extinguish his lamp continuously; the geographer who doesn't move from his books, waiting for explorers to tell him about the world. Grown-ups are extremely strange, thinks the little Prince with his pure childlike mind. They are so caught up in things that don't matter whereas the things that do, they don't even notice. They always ask how old someone is, how many brothers and sisters he has, not things like what games does he like, does he collect butterflies, what does his voice sound like?

A colorful lesson

The French animated cartoon film *Le Tableau* (The Painting) was made for children, too, although its message can also be taken to heart by a much wider audience. The core of the story is that the painter didn't finish a certain painting and the characters who had been completed consider themselves above those who were only partially finished and certainly way above those which were still in sketch form.

Obviously the underdogs want to remedy this situation and, accompanied by a young finished character, a *toupin* (which is a play on the words 'all painted' in French), who is in love with a partially painted girl, several of them take off in search of the painter to finish them so that every character in the painting can be equal. Their adventures have many lessons for us too as they tumble down into a war painting and rescue a little drummer boy, who's fed up with being involved in war for eternity, and as they meet and unmask Death.

Like *The Little Prince*, it is a parable of how certain adults behave and it is easy to see ourselves and many other people we've met in its beautifully drawn characters.

What's a birthday?

In *There's No Such Place as Far Away*, the narrator tells of flying to Rae's birthday party. She is a friend and is just turning 5. He meets a hummingbird and an owl who find the concept of a birthday, a party and a present very hard to understand. The owl tells him that if he wants to be with someone, surely he's already there. He cannot understand either why the narrator refers to his friend as 'little'. The eagle and the hawk are similarly puzzled.

They, too, wonder how she can have a birthday and why that should call for a celebration. In their view she must always have existed.

The narrator explains patiently that she's one more year away from childhood.

Hawk is astonished. His idea of 'growing up' certainly doesn't include the notion of leaving childhood behind.

It is only at the end of the story that the narrator finally understands; Rae has always existed and always will exist and he takes great comfort from that.

The joy of childhood

When we're children we can't wait to grow up and have the freedoms adults seem to have like eating ice cream every day and being allowed to leave the spinach on the side of our plate; like going to bed whenever we want and having all the toys we could possibly desire. It's such a pity when we hunger to put away childish things, because adulthood brings its own sorrows as well as joys and growing up too fast takes away the beautiful innocence that being a child should mean.

Traditions and Festivals

Every society has its own traditions and customs and celebrates its own festivals, some of which go back so far into the past that their origins are unknown. When people make their homes away from where they grew up they often recreate the customs in their new habitat. Going to Russia with my mother one Christmas exactly a year after my father died, we were not particularly pleased at the celebrations laid on for Christmas Day and New Year's Eve which we had traveled abroad in order to forget.

The winter solstice celebrations go back into the mists of time when the only light our ancestors had was daylight and fire, thus they were much more in tune with nature and the heavens; and when the shortest day came on 21 December and, on 22 and 23 December, night fell at exactly the same moment, the world seemed to be going into perpetual darkness. Imagine their joy on 24 December when a minute or two were added to the daylight and just marvel at how, with their closeness to nature, they were able to perceive the difference.

The origins of Yule

The festival of Yule itself comes to us from the Germanic peoples and the Wiccans and originally it celebrated the winter solstice. The ceremonies lasted for several days and involved a lot of drinking and debauchery (no change there then!). This was why the early Christian church, which obviously disapproved of such goings on, transformed Yule into a religious festival. The old ways have never really been forgotten and many people are returning to the beliefs and ceremonies of the past.

The Yule log is one of the few traditions left to us from that time. In fact we often call the season Yuletide. Many people don't really know the significance of the Yule log and neither did I until a shamanic practitioner explained it. To cleanse the home of evil spirits people took a log and wound strands of ivy round it. They put it on the open fire, often found in the entrance to their homes, and when the wood expanded and the strands exploded it was believed that the fire (which many shamanic traditions say cleanses and purifies) and the noise caused the evil spirits to leave the house and protected the inhabitants for another year.

Some traditions never die

Carol singing is a later tradition as singers have been out and about in England at the same time of year only since the Middle Ages when beggars would go round singing for food. As a teenager I used to go carol singing with a group outside. Then we would go round knocking on people's doors, collecting money for local charities.

At New Year there are many traditions, such as first-footing, and in Scotland the first person over the threshold of a house has to be a dark-haired male carrying a lump of coal for luck. Fair-haired men were traditionally associated with the Norse invaders and are still not welcome to first-foot.

A Japanese friend told me that at midnight on New Year's Eve in her country all the temple gongs chime. The origin of this, although also lost in the mists of time, is probably to chase away the evil spirits, too. In fact, even in space-clearing ceremonies, which are becoming better known in the West, a great deal of noise is made with gongs, bells and singing bowls to drive out the negative energies that have become trapped in the fabric of a building. When the clearing is over, the wishes of the inhabitants are read aloud and broadcast throughout the house, building, apartment or whatever has been treated, accompanied by the gentle tinkling of harmony balls.

The floral festival

The ancient tradition of Mothering Sunday has developed into Mothers' Day and this is a time when people traditionally buy flowers for their mothers. My own mother always insisted that it was related to the mothering of the church and she was right.

Several centuries ago, on the fourth Sunday in Lent, people went back to their local or mother church and this particularly applied to domestic servants. With their mothers they went to the church in the area where they were brought up, and as they would be needed to work at holidays such as Christmas, it was often the only day they had off to visit their families. The tradition of giving flowers probably came from picking wild flowers on the way back to their home villages, either for the church or for the mothers, and it is sad that children now have no idea of the origins of the custom and are urged to buy flowers at inflated prices.

Going further back

If we go back to Celtic times we find the festivals of Beltane and Samhain; in fact they are words derived from Gaelic. Beltane was celebrated on the first day of May and fires were always lit on the hills as a means of purification and blessing. The May Queen was crowned and Tennyson wrote a poem about a girl asking her mother to wake her early as she was to be Queen of the May. In the Catholic tradition, this has become the day of the Virgin Mary.

Samhain is a Gaelic festival to celebrate the harvest which was never fixed although it marked the change of seasons. Pope Gregory in the eighth century decided it should be on 31 October to coincide with All Souls' Day in the Christian calendar. It is said that the night of Samhain is when the veil between the two worlds is at its thinnest and again bonfires are lit. It was a time of slaughter, for people to lay in and preserve meat for the winter, and masks were worn to ward off those evil spirits which seem to pop up everywhere in many of these traditions. The children would go round with lanterns made from pumpkins and offer entertainment in exchange for food or coins.

These festivals have continued with few changes throughout the centuries and it is heartening to find that people are beginning to take an interest again, to learn what they originally celebrated and to bring them back for us to enjoy.

Two Little Words

Walking down Oxford Street, the main London shopping thoroughfare, one Saturday morning as the shops were opening I came across a man carrying a mop and bucket giving directions to a tourist. As I drew level with them he turned and stomped off, yelling: 'You could at least say "thank you". It's only two little words.'

The lady looked completely bemused but managed to mutter a 'thank you' to his retreating back.

Perhaps not a typical example, but I do notice when I go into the local bakery here in Geneva that quite a few customers say neither 'please' nor 'thank you'. Customs differ and I have had to learn to preface any query to a bus driver, an enquiry desk official, a supermarket employee, etc. with a *Bonjour*, whereas in the UK we would say: 'Excuse me, can you tell me ...?' You say that too of course, but you have to start any conversation, query, complaint, whatever, with a *Bonjour* if you don't want the person you're addressing turning, hands on hips, giving you a loud and loaded *BONJOUR*. 'Thank you' must be fairly universal, but is it going out of fashion? Do people have so much on their minds that they don't have time for what used to be considered plain courtesy?

Do we always remember?

And what about us? Is there anybody who doesn't appreciate what transactional analysis, so fashionable in the 1980s, called 'strokes'? Recently I had an e-mail from a colleague who wanted some information he thought I might have. He left his phone number and I called him back. I've known him for a long time and he has gone through some really tough moments in his life. We talked about many things for well over half an hour and I was not only amazed but thrilled to receive a short e-mail afterwards, thanking me for just being there. I didn't feel I had done anything special at all but my colleague obviously did and his thoughtful message made me feel great.

If we are invited for a meal or to a party, do we systematically send an e-mail or text the next day to thank the host? If we receive a little present do we immediately contact the sender to express our appreciation; even if it's something we're going to pass on as fast as we can because it's not to our taste? No matter, the giver has thought of us.

Making it a habit

We all have so much of everything, but do we focus on being grateful for what we do have or rather on the things we want? It doesn't need to have a religious connotation either. If I have an outdoor activity planned I'm extremely pleased when the sun shines and a 'thank you' to it is a reflex action. Picking up a coin in the street, receiving a kind message, having things go better than expected, someone sending an invitation out of the blue, an evening spent chatting with good friends, a new job assignment, they're all occasions to put a 'thank you' out into the ethers. At the end of every day I say 'thank you' that all my needs have been met; not necessarily all my wants; that's quite a different matter. We've got this far in life and, even with the bumps and wounds and heartache we pick up on the journey and which are part of the human experience, we've come through and there's no reason to believe that will ever change.

Meister Eckhart, a medieval mystic and theologian, put it even higher. One of his best-known sayings is this: *If the only prayer you say in your whole life is 'thank you', that would suffice.*

It is said that love makes the world go round, but love and gratitude are both very positive energies and a world without gratitude would be as sterile as a world without love.

About the Author

Jili Hamilton was born in England and has done a variety of jobs, including secretarial work, office administration, translating, bookselling, waitressing and chamber-maiding. She also worked as a listener for the Samaritans in Switzerland (*La main tendue*) and Belgium (*Télé-accueil*) for over five years and has obtained a diploma in hypnotherapy. Jili has studied many aspects of self-development and bodywork, starting out with the Godefroy method of Alpha Dynamics and following it up with the Silva Method, both in 1989. She has facilitated courses in intuition and how to develop it as well as how to improve one's life through positive thinking and specific techniques.

At present working as a teacher, therapist, proof-reader and translator, she lives in Switzerland. Jili understands that listening is a very important part of healing and always starts her sessions (which are for donation only) by encouraging those who consult her to endeavor to look more closely at what isn't working in their lives and to see with them what they can do to change things.

Jili has also edited a book entitled *Messages from beyond the Veil*, containing spirit writings by her grandmother who was a channel and medium and which is available from http://www.amazon.co.uk. She is currently rewriting *Hopi Candles*, her book on ear treatment candles, and it will be available shortly. The French version, which is in its third edition, is published by Indigo-Montangero under the title *Les bougies auriculaires et leurs bienfaits méconnus*.

You may wish to visit her website (www.jilihamilton.com) or contact her by e-mail (info@jilihamilton.com) with any questions or comments; she really enjoys receiving feedback and sharing as much information as possible.

BOOKS

O is a symbol of the world, of oneness and unity. In different cultures it also means the "eye," symbolizing knowledge and insight. We aim to publish books that are accessible, constructive and that challenge accepted opinion, both that of academia and the "moral majority."

Our books are available in all good English language bookstores worldwide. If you don't see the book on the shelves ask the bookstore to order it for you, quoting the ISBN number and title. Alternatively you can order online (all major online retail sites carry our titles) or contact the distributor in the relevant country, listed on the copyright page.

See our website **www.o-books.net** for a full list of over 500 titles, growing by 100 a year.

And tune in to myspiritradio.com for our book review radio show, hosted by June-Elleni Laine, where you can listen to the authors discussing their books.

mySpiritRadio